THE SECRET
of INNER PRESENCE

THE SECRET
of INNER PRESENCE

Keys to Awaken Inner Presence,
to Transform Your Life and the Global Community

LIN LIPETZ

iUniverse, Inc.
Bloomington

THE SECRET OF INNER PRESENCE
Keys to Awaken Inner Presence, to Transform Your Life and the Global Community

iUniverse books may be ordered through booksellers or by contacting:

iUniverse
1663 Liberty Drive
Bloomington, IN 47403
www.iuniverse.com
1-800-Authors (1-800-288-4677)

ISBN: 978-1-4759-0172-6 (sc)
ISBN: 978-1-4759-0171-9 (hc)
ISBN: 978-1-4759-0170-2 (ebk)

Library of Congress Control Number: 2012904945

Printed in the United States of America

iUniverse rev. date: 04/30/2012

CONTENTS

FOREWORD

"The Secret of Inner Presence is about one person's choice to communicate very personally with the intelligence of the Universe that is constantly available. She is inspired to share the truth of this communication and connection with others to go beyond themselves into a state of higher knowing and inner love and light, through the power of Inner Presence. We welcome the opportunity to begin what has become a profound and inspirational book of Universal knowledge. This kind of knowledge can only be received by those willing to search for what is hidden from normal consciousness. It is available to all, but it takes patience and trust to go beyond what is usually experienced during the human life.

It is our hope that each of you reading this book will choose to follow these teachings until you too are an integral part of the loving Universe of all intelligence and celestial beings. The way to our loving essence is presented creatively through an artist of the heart to whom we have given our love, with the expectation that this spiritual pathway that she has experienced will be released into the world for the benefit of all.

We are in every word of the book and assist you in each chapter as you go within to find Inner Presence, your constant divine Source of love. The power for the magnification of this Source of true peace and joy throughout life is inside you right now, just waiting to be turned on!

Love is the Heart of the Universe

There is an invisible Universe that loves and cares for each person on this planet. It loves and cares for everything it has made. It connects to you through your core-self, the soul. Ask for its love and it will respond. Its name is love spoken in a thousand different tongues because love is the heart of the Universe. Feel its sweetest warmth in your heart, its caress in your mind."

_____God, Frieda and Valto and the Spiritual Universe

DEDICATION

I dedicate this book to my daughter Jan Lipetz
and my son Brad Lipetz. They are my best
friends and the loves of my life.

ACKNOWLEDGEMENTS

I wish to greatly thank the Universe for transforming my life through the magic of my awakening to the knowledge of Inner Presence. I also want to thank my spiritual guides Frieda and Valto, and the spiritual Universe for giving me the ability to receive their messages. I am so very thankful to be chosen as a messenger to carry their words forward into the world.

My many, many thanks to Jackie Lee for her constant support and her willingness to be the main editor of this book. I would also like to thank Dorna Andersen and Francoise Jacot for their editorial reviews, and for their continuing advice whenever it was needed.

There are many friends of *The Secret of Inner Presence,* but I would particularly like to thank Rayne Dessayer, Lucy Hamlyn, Ann Hollister, Roni Kalyk and Lonni Pristovock for their belief in me and their best wishes for the success of the book and its message.

INTRODUCTION

To make this spiritual journey, you will need to leave your analytical mind behind—and travel with an open heart!

The Secret of Inner Presence speaks through messages received from the consciousness of the Universe with profound insights that can transform your life and empower you to live at a much higher level of awareness. Throughout the book, in this journey towards oneself, the mind sinks into the heart and you become aware of a central-core divine Inner Presence that is always unchangeably and lovingly present. It is an invisible Presence of love and light that has always been available, perhaps without your awareness. Once you awaken this core-self at a new and higher level of consciousness, you will find that many of your patterns of thought and perception begin to change. Life becomes beautifully smooth and glowing as you learn to commune with this divine love that now lives in your heart. Throughout the book you are guided step by step with constant caring instruction from the Universe and the author's personal experience of spiritual transformation through her illuminating experiences with Inner Presence. It offers the way for a new internal view of oneself where the riches of the heart and the soul lie.

So many, many people are totally unaware of the vast amount of knowledge and beauty that is forever available within. There is so much more to know and to become when your magnificent spirits are called into full expression. If the door could just be opened and the misty veils removed for "clear inner sight" it would a true miracle. It has taken many years for me to realize that I have been entrusted with keys to assist in opening these thin, thin doors for others and to help remove many of the veils that are just waiting to be lifted. This knowledge was given to me by the consciousness of the Universe during my awakening twenty-five years ago and I have been instructed that I am to now be the creative messenger to help show others "the way that I was given," through a series of spiritual key steps that are completely described throughout the book. These keys are offered to consciously open your awareness to the knowledge of Inner Presence, your soul essence, your God force. As you learn to recognize this Presence and live within that higher frequency, you will move into a whole new way of living that will gradually transform your life and possibly the world community as well.

The amazing experience that opened my inner eyes to the vastness of this available knowledge and constant love is described in the story of my spiritual awakening in the first chapter. Please begin there because it sets the stage for each of the following chapters. I suggest that you read each one sequentially for the greatest understanding and growth. Together all the chapters represent the transformational journey I have experienced while living with the nurturing guidance of Inner Presence, my guides and the consciousness of the Universe through the years. I am so incredibly thankful to have been given this incredible experience that was just waiting to be perceived.

Much of the instruction and information I have received in the messages from the loving caring entities in the Universe over the years, is divided into four separate chapters and it is also presented in several of the other chapters for more complete clarification. All of this material has been given to me through my dialogues with the Universe during stream of consciousness writing sessions and while in the process of writing this book. Right now, this minute, I "feel" that the Universe would like to speak:

> "The entire Universe is a conscious living colossus. Constellations, fundamental elements and substances,

master teachers, all that pass from birth to death, all the many, many galaxies—are one homogenous whole, interacting and communicating in a multiplicity of ways. Everything on earth was created from this seed of consciousness and all together it is what you call God, or Source, the Universal mind, or Love. This living-breathing life force Universe that you constantly interact with, is both too complex and too simple for the mind to grasp—but it is intuitively felt when going within the self for communication and contemplation. You can then receive the teachers and guidance you ask for and they can be addressed as friends in familiar endearing terms. You will feel the interaction because we are truly one entity living within each other. We breathe along with you within our own space-time orbit.

Human beings are here on this planet to grow into the fullness of their soul light. To know whence they came remains a mystery. It is enough to know in your earth life that there is beneficent interaction and that it is constantly available. The choice is always yours: To seek further inner connection with the living Universe to become much more than your present self, or to stay within your present self and grow at the accepted level of earth space-time.

Going into Inner Presence is like entering a special form of learning that is a part of every person's psyche. It is easily accessed, just waiting to be discovered. Opening to this level of knowledge is a privilege. When you flow your being into the consciousness of the Universe it combines with new dimensions of knowledge and guidance that have been unknown to you before. Flow into this domain easily through the strength of pure love that always resides in the heart. This is the pathway to open to our divine living Presence, the God frequency, which is ever available when you learn that this higher level actually exists. Let yourselves be guided to uncover the secret of Inner Presence through the spiritual pathway provided by *one who knows the way. Once connected, the opening into this vast wisdom of your many guiding teachers will forever be available. As you open to this new dimension within yourselves we ask you to share this knowledge with others, so that the awareness of our Presence continues to multiply."*

The promises of this book are to help make readers aware of the interactive loving life force of our Universe, and to help awaken divine Inner Presence in the human heart. For those already on a personal spiritual path, my hope is that what is offered here will be a very helpful and useful guide. Because *The Secret of Inner Presence* was written to be both experienced and practiced, you may want to start by reading it all the way through for a better understanding of the overall content before beginning your own personal journey. Several of the chapters end with a document in your journal section. Because spiritual work is often about ephemeral feelings and emotions that may be difficult to remember, they really need to be captured immediately, preferably in writing. You will find that documenting is almost a necessity for understanding your spiritual growth.

As a visual artist and teacher, I have always been interested in the process of how something is made and the series of steps along the way toward completion. When reading books I like to know how and why the basic information is gathered so I, the reader, can understand the background story and therefore trust its truth. For this reason, in the Appendix I have included some of the entries from my journals that were written about living with Inner Presence and my invisible guides and teachers.

How to Use this Book

Whenever the Universe speaks throughout the book it is always presented in *italic font.*

Because I use the word God, or God force, throughout the book, this may be difficult for many of you, but please do not let semantics become a block. Substitute whatever feels right—Presence, Source,

Tao, Allah, Goddess, Spirit. As you will read in the messages, our divine Source does not care about specific names.

The Universe Speaks

Love is the Heart of the Universe

Introduction: *"This book is given to all who choose to open the doors beyond their normal everyday selves to find another world of inner love, and to explore the spiritual resources that are ever available and waiting.*

WAITING

This is the now of the
Universe, waiting and
Waiting for you to appear,
To give you what is rightly
Yours to become more fulfilled.

We can, if you let us,
Transform your life."

CHAPTER ONE

MY SPIRITUAL AWAKENING

The Discovery of Inner Presence

The first key to the Secret of Inner Presence is the discovery that this divine center lives within each and every human being just waiting to be discovered, either gradually over perhaps a period of years through spiritual desire, through the emotion of peaceful love, or spontaneously, as with my story below.

My Spiritual History

Before relating the story of my spiritual awakening it may be helpful to know something of my on-again, off-again spiritual life. When I was a child my mother took me to the Presbyterian Sunday school in Bozeman, Montana and as I grew older we regularly attended church there. All through those growing up years I daily prayed to God as my very special friend and decided early on that the Bible stories of being born in sin were totally false. I earnestly believed in a beneficent and loving God. Later, mother began to attend the Christian Science Church and after retiring from her administrative

1

job she daily retreated for a while to her bedroom to read Unity magazine. Often I would read those daily lessons myself and they gradually opened my mind to explore new ways of thinking about faith, religion and spirituality.

As a young mother I took my children to a Presbyterian Sunday school in Seattle, Washington and actively participated in the church until the minister literally removed the life size nativity scene I had created for a live evening Christmas pageant. The next day, without explanation, the wooden structure, the crib and the straw had all disappeared because it hid the pulpit. The minister came to our home to empathize with my concerns, but did not apologize, so I rarely went back—having lost all belief in ministers being more elevated spiritually than the rest of us. I decided to find my own way and began attending the Unitarian Church in Seattle, and later the Christian Science Church in Sonoma and the Napa Valley Center for Living based on the Science of Mind book and teachings of Ernest Holmes. There were also occasional visits to Zen Centers for meditation. I now realize that this rather haphazard but very real desire for spiritual growth finally led to my spiritual awakening.

The Awakening that Transformed my Life

In the winter of 1986 I was happy and content with no intention of beginning to live more spiritually, until I was suddenly awakened to the awareness of an inner shimmering Presence that began to live in my heart in the twinkling of an eye when I least expected it. I just knew that receiving it was the most magical event of my life and I have cherished it like a precious jewel in my heart ever since. It is my nurturing secret place to intuitively open for love, peace, creativity and spiritual guidance whenever I am in harmony with its vibrations. I tell my story here at the beginning of the book as an introduction to the amazing inner joy and love you will receive as you work with each chapter of this book.

On a rainy day I drove up to Sonoma from San Jose, California for an exhibition of my paintings. That night, after the opening, I stayed alone in my friend's historic stone studio just off the Plaza. She is both an aesthetician and astrologer, so it was a most interesting place to stay, with her art, astrology charts and spiritual posters everywhere displayed on the walls and ceiling. Thinking back to that night, it seems to me now that I must have been feeling a bit strange, and maybe a little lonely. The lampshade glowed a soft pink comforting light as I sat there looking languidly around at all the images and textiles she had so carefully collected. Then gradually I began thinking about love and what it is—why I am not sure. I had always thought of love as involving another person, someone to love or to be loved by. So, thinking this way I began to wonder lazily if love could be experienced without the involvement of someone else? Could one generate the emotion of being in love within oneself? How would I do that?

Deciding to experiment with this idea I simply looked up at a ceiling poster of Swami Muktananda whispering inwardly, "I Love You God" and projected that feeling of being totally in love with another person upward from my heart. Almost instantly warm vibrant currents of love's energy flowed up into the image directly from my heart. Amazingly, the feeling I felt was absolutely identical with actually being in love! Then, still looking up I said, "I Love Myself". Immediately those same rays of love rushed right back to me, joyously plunging deeply into my heart pinning me to the chair with their intensity! My body felt illuminated, the room seemed to pulse with light and I sat there totally embraced in a sea of love. It felt as if a miracle had just happened!! There is no other way to describe this experience except to say that afterwards for a long time it seemed as if I was floating within invisible arms of total loving bliss. Gradually, much later, in a quiet happy kind of daze I thanked God for what had been given to me, and crawled into bed, immediately drifting peacefully off to sleep.

The next day, awakening into the bright, clear sunlit morning with birds singing outside the windows, I felt a stirring of exquisite secret happiness breaking softly into my awareness. Had something truly magical happened last night or was it simply a beautiful dream? Why had I decided to experiment with love anyway? Afraid, and not afraid to test for answers before getting up I closed my eyes, tentatively saying again inwardly "I Love You God" and immediately the same waves of warmth that I had felt the night before radiated within my heart. I then inwardly said, "I Love Myself." And those waves of invisible energy grew even stronger; filling my entire body with pure loving beauty that was both exciting and somehow very, very, peaceful. With certainty then, I knew and accepted that I had received the knowledge that love can be experienced without the involvement of another and it can be equally as beautiful! I blinked, amazed at this new knowledge. Finally after dressing, I walked around Sonoma Plaza and the town all day long, secretly so very joyous, holding within this precious treasure of my inner miracle. Later that day driving back to San Jose I felt a total sense of completeness. I also felt intuitively that because something profoundly significant had happened to me that I must nurture and develop its Presence; otherwise it would simply wither quietly away and be lost!

During the following weeks and months I quietly meditated and really began for the first time to understand what loving one's self truly meant. The simple truth of my own human and divine perfection began to glide slowly into consciousness. I began to open to loving others in new unconditional ways that I had never done before and listened with greater interest and respect to the many stories of their lives. Gradually my life became much more fulfilling as I listened and learned inwardly during the daily meditations that expanded and strengthened what I had been given. All shyness, fear of leadership, fear of the past, and uncertainty about the future vanished, as I trusted more and more that I was now much more than myself in an effortless transformation. For a long time I felt powerless to give this new feeling a name, until I finally decided to call it "Heart-Warmth Energy," because gentle heat always began there—right in the center. Later I began to envision this heat as a small golden flame that I could project outward and tried to live in its awareness throughout each day. To practice, I would bring its warm vibrations to the surface of my attention on walks, during yoga, while driving, etc. For all these years now, this flame in my heart has been a constant loving Presence that I know will be with me for the rest of my life—if I continue to tend it well!

I now call this feeling "Inner Presence" because it does feel that way. There are still times when I cannot call it forth because my thoughts are too busy wind milling around or I am focused on something else. This also happens occasionally during meditation when I have not scheduled enough time, or I just can't seem to "get there." I used to fret about this but now I simply thank myself for moving into the silence for a while, knowing "just sitting" is of greatest importance as I continue to learn to live more harmoniously within the essence of this divine nurturing.

Beginning Stream of Consciousness Writing

A few years later in 2001 I began to desire more knowledge about the spiritual world that had touched me so purposefully. I decided to experiment with visualization techniques, lucid dreaming, intuition and channeling voices, but nothing happened. One day as I was looking at the several Edgar Cayce books in my library I opened once again, *Edgar Cayce, On Channeling Your Higher Self,* by Henry Reed and read the chapter on Inspirational Writing that included information about automatic and stream of consciousness writing. "Well, why not try it," I thought," wondering if it would really work if I just set pencil to paper, letting words flow forth unconsciously in a kind of fuzzy semi-conscious state as described in the book?"

During the very first session I was amazed to see that entire sentences did in fact appear even though they were quite meaningless, except for a few complete statements here and there. Gradually after a week or two of this kind of practice I decided to begin each session with a written question, meditate briefly, and then wait quietly without the expectation of a response. This relaxed passivity and focus on a particular subject did prove to be the key to unlock a really abundant flow of inner whispered answers that I began to call dialogues. Amazingly I had found my personal key to discover what I began to think of as "Unlocking Secrets of the Universe."

When I first began writing questions the responses were from "I" or "We." Now, I know that God spoke as "I" and my guides spoke as "We." Later as this inner exchange continued I asked if spiritual guides had names and to my amazement they answered,

> "Yes, we are guides from the higher realms with the names of Frieda and Valto."

Since that beginning Frieda and Valto and I have continued to develop the loving bond that I could not now, ever do without! They are constantly available whenever I choose to sit down for a writing session, or to listen internally wherever I am. Throughout our many silent discussions their whispered messages are unconditionally loving, sometimes very funny, occasionally chiding, but definitely written from their perspective of another reality. I sincerely hope you will get to know your own invisible spirit guides as you develop a deeper continuing relationship with the vast number of intelligences in our loving Universe.

Creative Results of My Spiritual Awakening

My passion has always been creativity through painting, ceramics, textile constructions, designing homes, or teaching people to be more creative through the visual arts. I had not expected another form of creativity to emerge, but almost immediately after receiving the gift of my awakening and beginning meditation I began to want to write. It seemed imperative to try to describe the ineffable as clearly as possible to make it more real and understandable to myself. Writing in my journal each day recording my spiritual experiences became a necessary and joyful part of my life. Then little poems began to emerge about bits and pieces of my day, the mood of a morning, or a frog just sitting, or a hovering hummingbird. In a way I began to feel that I was feeding the light in my soul to let it shine forth in new ways that I had never considered before.

Later, the messages that I continued to receive through stream of consciousness writing taught me that energy and breath are constantly feeding everything with Universal life energy that is ever present and constantly flowing and circling, nurturing everything on earth with spiritual sustenance. One morning in the summer of 2008 I sat down in my studio, and brought the warmth of Inner Presence into my awareness. Then just sitting in a quiet meditative state I began trying to interpret energy and breath visibly, sweeping it in and around simple little line drawings of water and sky in a rather abstract way. Each day I could hardly wait to experiment further and began adding the beauty of transparent watercolor. The result was radically different than all my previous abstract work. Gradually the desire to depict this invisible circulation of energy became the heart of my paintings. Also stories emerged magically as I drew, and I found that if a painting needed something realistic, like a bird or dragonfly, I could depict each one quite easily, something I had never been able to do before. At the same time I became more trusting of my intuition in new ways, letting it totally guide me, which led to teaching Intuitive Painting. So I now encourage my students to use intuition as their guide to reveal their own intrinsic creativity in new ways that includes the circulation of energy and unique inner stories.

The presence of my Intuitive Paintings in this book is intended to express the mystery of our Universe in another way, and to see the evidence of Inner Presence and creative transformation actualized. I am so thankful to the Universe for the guidance to grow further and further in the direction of my own passions. It is also very clear that this can be true for everyone. So this book, in collaboration with the Universe, is my desire to transmit what I know to be true.

The Meaning of Inner Presence and Heart-Warmth Energy

As you have read in my awakening story above, the two phrases I used to describe the internal feeling of that gift were, "inner shimmering presence" and "heart-warmth energy". It gradually became known to me that inner shimmering presence should be called Inner Presence. I have asked the Universe for the descriptions of both Inner Presence and Heart-Warmth Energy:

> "Inner Presence (our Creator's Presence within)
>> I am your Creator, your Inner Presence and always have been. Until awakened I am not felt as a being within, I am out of sight, so to speak. When I am awakened, you become aware of my Presence because my energy is vibrating. I combine All that I Am with your humanness. I am your fulcrum, your center of all beauty and light. I am the way! Open to my love and knowledge for it will carry

you far to your greatest joy and achievements throughout life. Inner Presence is my sparkling shimmering self that will give you all that you seek.

Heart-Warmth Energy (our Creator's Presence within the heart) Heart-warmth energy is very real and beautiful and may be used to describe Inner Presence. They can be used together or separately for I am both. I speak from within the heart with my energy and love that also warms in wavelengths of heat and light. You can feel the vibrations of my energy and see it as it drifts outside the body in rays of color."

Transformational Experiences—Quotes

I have read many books that draw on the writings of Western and Eastern spiritual traditions to help me understand the awakening experience with greater clarity and to find others who have had similar experiences. In Ralph Metzner's book, *Unfolding Within: Varieties of Transformative Experience,* there are a great number of examples that have beautifully answered my questions and I have listed a few below for your reference. It is fascinating that these descriptions of transformation, Inner Presence, lifting veils of illusion, inner light and heart warmth are all typical of the awakening experience regardless of the historical period or cultural background.

Dr. Ralph Metzner, *Unfolding Within*:

"The transformation may be abrupt or gradual. Ecstasy, peak experience, inspired revelation, flash of inventive insight, the poet's vision—all these are sudden experiences that may bring about profound changes in a person's life" (15).

"The transformation may be externally or internally induced by an accident, sight of natural wonders, contact with another or love at first sight. An external person catalyzing a transformation is typically a guru or spiritual teacher. Baptism, shaktipat, transmission of power, Tantric Hinduism, hypnosis all are ritualized forms of externally induced alteration" (15).

"Experiences of heightened consciousness, of mystical oneness or rapture, may be accompanied by a sense of their having been given freely and unexpectedly through God's grace" (16).

"A person no longer has the sense of separateness, even in ordinary, everyday consciousness" (18).

"When we awaken in a spiritual sense we become aware of an Essence, the Self that is immortal and omnipresent. We are urged to awaken to the divine nature inherently within" (33).

"Veils of illusion are like clouds of unknowing between you and your God. These are the clouds of the unconsciousness that blocks the light of the inner sun, the light of spirit" (38).

"Everything we look at in such states seems illuminated with a kind of pristine luminous beauty comparable to the light of a new day dawning" (38).

"Spiritual transformation has been described as a change from outer to inner focus, from the material world of the senses to the spiritual worlds revealed by inner sight. It is also a shift from the familiar world of space and time to the transcendent worlds where everything appears as it is—infinite" (43).

"The medieval theologians taught that we have the eye of the flesh which sees worldly things, the eye of reason by which we know the mind and concepts, and the eye of contemplation by which we know transcendent, spiritual realities. The way of true wisdom involved the ability to consciously function with and differentiate these three sources of knowledge" (45).

"For European alchemists, Chinese Taoists and shamanic native cultures the world of Spirit and the world of nature are unified, not separated as in Western rationalist mentality" (79).

The fourteenth-century English mystic Richard Rolle, in his tract *The Fire of Love*, gives this account: "I cannot tell you how surprised I was the first time I felt my heart begin to warm. It was real warmth, too, not imaginary and it felt as if it were actually on fire. I was astonished at the way the heat surged up and how this new sensation brought great and unexpected comfort. It set my soul aglow as if a real fire were burning there" (91).

"The light and heat in the soul's core overflows into the body which becomes radiant with it. This light-fire energy is often perceived as healing as well as spiritually illuminating. The light or energy is felt as suffusing the interior of the body bringing deep feelings of love and tremendous well being" (163).

"In the state of illumination light seems to pour through the body and flow outward. The eyes radiate, the face shines and the heart 'sees.' Experiences of the heart center opening are accompanied by sensations of warmth, openness and lightness" (164).

"Each human being is in essence a divine spirit of pure light. This light can come 'down' or 'through' into mind and body, into outward expression and manifestation. Christian mystics and theologians make it abundantly clear that light is not an abstract symbol but an actual energy that is known in the mind, felt in the heart, sensed in the body, and that comes from, and is, Spirit" (169).

Sri Aurobindo, *The Life Divine*, "The light of divine Spirit may occur spontaneously and unexpectedly, and with the dawning of the inner light of Spirit/Self a new and higher level of consciousness is initiated. The individual is now fired with 'God force,' connected to the divine Source or ground of all life" (173).

CHAPTER TWO

DOCUMENT YOUR EXPERIENCES

Journals

This second key introduces you to a practical record keeping process of your spiritual journey. This diary will become a most appreciated silent companion as you continue along your way to connection with Inner Presence and inner transformation.

Writing about your spiritual experiences throughout this book is a way to accurately record what was most important in the moment. For that reason there is a reminder at the end of several of the chapters to document in your journal. For those of you who are new to journal writing I hope the following information will be helpful.

Journals are very important in my life, to document precious thoughts, daily rituals, instructions, and to save special bits and pieces of information. When in a new learning cycle I look forward eagerly to entering my observations and experiences at the end of each day in those personal pages where I can explore my mind and heart freely without interference. It is a private time where I can say what I wish, without censure, create a record of special events and also feel the support of the journal as a silent companion.

As you begin or continue your journal writing, these records will be constant friends of your inner travels throughout life, preserving and honoring your deepest thoughts without judgment. They are also a wonderful place to explore writing expressively and authentically, all that you think and feel and desire. In the information below you will find a description of three journals, a quick and visual documentation system and some notes about writing. Whether writing with pencil and paper or on the computer, you can use the same organizing and drawing processes.

The Process

Types of Journals

I suggest using a standard 3-ring binder and dividers for each chapter. This is the journal you will use if you are writing on an ongoing basis, as it is big enough to contain all your personal material. You may also want to have pockets in the binder for clippings, and scotch tape available for pictures, etc. As you continue you will be amazed at the flashes of intuition you will begin to notice or new information that will be revealed in your writing. It may be that you will have sat in meditation for a half hour in the morning, with nothing seemingly happening, and yet by evening you will realize you have much to report about the session itself, or the insights you received later as you went about your day.

It is also helpful to have a second small "thought catcher" notebook to quickly jot down brief special insights that might otherwise slip away unnoticed. Any generic notebook with lined paper and a hard cover is perfect for this. I also suggest a third small travel journal to carry in your pocket or purse. Because I like to personalize things, mine is called "Flowing Lines from the Mind and Heart," and I do try to use it that way. Although it is usually a mess of briefly described jottings quickly caught, when I get home after being out all day, these small bits of information take me back to the moment, coaxing those quiet thoughts back to life. All three of these notebooks fit the categories of inexpensive and easy to find. You, of course, may prefer the more beautifully bound journals. I simply suggest, whatever you choose, that you write in them regularly. I have several unlined beauties that friends have given me, all still empty. So my thoughts are these, small journals are too cramped for expansive thinking and writing, unlined books become a mess, and expensive journals stay empty—waiting for a few moments of word magic that may never happen.

Documentation

These years of writing have taught me to use a simple system to easily search and find specific information at a later date. At the beginning of each writing day, note the day of the week, month, year and page number at the top of the page. Maybe you will also want to indicate the time you begin and then some basic facts of your day or what you had for breakfast or whatever tumbles out. In this way, as you work with each chapter, you will have established how it is for you that day, a very important part of the investigative process you are now involved in. Maybe you have read an article or book that you want to refer to later, so note the page and sentence. You will be so glad you did when trying to remember where you read that perfect quote.

When you have finished for the day make brief concise summaries at the top for easy reference, possibly highlighting especially important information. Writing these headlines forces you to draw conclusions that can lead to expanded thinking and also serve as your search-and-find road maps throughout your journals. You may think all of this attention to details is very picky but you will thank yourself later when you are going through many pages of writing, knowing the year, possibly the date but only a hazy recollection of your thinking at that time. Looking through the heading summaries will save hours of work shuffling through the many pages.

Writing

Let us talk about writing for a while. These notebooks are for your eyes only, so correct grammar; spelling and complete sentences are unnecessary. To keep the writing from becoming a time consuming drudgery you will find using abbreviations and eliminating verbs will provide the same meaning as a complete sentence. An example of a full description would be: "Jan and I went to see the Shakespeare stage play at Gundlach Bundschu winery last night. We loved it, a wonderful performance. She was not herself all evening though, and I still don't know why." Maybe the complete description of the event is important because it is the highlight of the day. Could you eliminate words and still keep the meaning? A shorthand description might be: "Jan & I Shakespeare play last nite, GB winery, loved it, Jan not herself, why?" Does the bare bones description still retain the meaning?

If you read *My Journals* at the end of the book, you will notice I often use this partially abbreviated method in an attempt to describe things quickly before the essence of the experience is lost. Learning to write briefly and concisely to capture the exact meaning in one word or sentence also stimulates the mind. And it is fun to do.

Identification Symbols and Drawings

Using colored pencils to enhance your drawings of daily weather symbols and simple line drawings of images you want to remember is both fun and beautiful and an immediate reminder of that time and place. Perhaps you were at the beach indicated with just a few blue wavy lines, or you took a walk in the forest remembered with a green tree or two. It is amazing how quickly little colored images will draw you back to that exact time and place. None of your drawings has to be pretty, because each one simply serves as a shorthand visual note to your memory. I do suggest they all be in a vertical row on the left side of the writing for easy reference. If you are documenting on your computer you can still draw in the margins later. I have to admit that I am a pencil and paper person and like to write, draw and color all at the same time. We each have our own way of working. The most important part is to have the materials you need in a private area where you can write easily and comfortably.

A Monthly Marker Day

At the end of each month of journaling, review your daily summaries at the top of each page and write a final monthly summary as exactly as possible. Include your ideas, your feelings, what you have learned, and what, if anything, you want to discard. If there are changes or desires or problem areas that need addressing, write them down as clearly and concisely as you can. Try to write only one short sentence for each desire, change or concern. Tightening those descriptions to only 4 or 5 words each is a great help in learning to be exact about what you are describing or feeling. On this marker day imagine another part of yourself as an observer, viewing your life and thoughts with greater detachment. What would your observer-self say?

Journal for the Next Chapter

Please have your large binder journal ready before beginning the next chapter. Your documented personal story will then faithfully reflect back what is most important to you from the very beginning of your Inner Presence spiritual journey.

CHAPTER THREE

AWAKEN INNER PRESENCE

Love

The Universe speaks: *"Awaken the truth of your connection to God, the Universe of All That Is. The connecting factor is love. Love is the Living Heart of the Universe! It has been given to each of you to use throughout your lives. Those of you who choose to create from love, to learn to know it well, will become light filled, expanding all that you are—into all that you can be."*

This third key is the most important key because it opens our conscious awareness to Inner Presence, the God force. We each have within ourselves this higher liberating level of consciousness that has been with us and available since birth. Occasionally we experience this transcending feeling when we go beyond our normal selves during highly emotional occasions where "something else" seems to take over unexpectedly, or during prayer or meditation, or when we are in nature or a place where we feel a sense of awe. We know we have this capacity to have these exalting experiences but we do not know that we can live at this higher immortal soul level of Inner Presence consistently.

How do we open our connection to divine Inner Presence? For some people there is a spontaneous mystical experience, as in the individual stories in this chapter and my own story. For others it may occur quite gradually from an experience in nature or cultivated by religious and spiritual practices. But ultimately for all seekers it is through love that the connection is finally made. Because we each have been given the ability to love, we can use this emotion that we know so well, to awaken the connection to our Inner Presence. The Universe has given us "the way" through the introduction above and the following simple and beautiful meditations. Once awakened, the God force that is Inner Presence will become the cornerstone of our lives. We will experience each and every day the way it transforms the very center of our being through love of self and all else. The intuitive guidance and inner messages we will continuously receive will always be aligned with our innate abilities, because each one of us is so unique in the world. As we harmonize both our human and divine selves more equally there is an "inner knowing" that we are whole and complete, and there is the constant of inner peace and contentment.

> *"Our Human and Divine Natures*
>> *You each have a human and divine nature that must be fully utilized and balanced to create the most of what your earth life offers. You all know the experience of living from your human mind, body and soul, but learning to expand your divine nature is necessary for complete fulfillment of all that you were given at birth. Awakening to your divine self through the emotion of peaceful love allows for the full blossoming of your divinity. It can also be opened more gradually through prayer, empathy with nature, and love of a particular place."*

Awaken Through Peaceful Love

The secret of awakening your Inner Presence begins with a daily ritual of the following peaceful love meditations given by the Universe. For at least two weeks faithfully meditate three times a day for ten minutes, possibly just before arising in the morning, during the day whenever possible, and at night just before drifting off to sleep. Each day this will become easier and more rewarding, but if at times it is difficult, just breathe deeply a few times and let the feelings of peaceful love drift in and around your body for awhile without meditating. Just let go and let Inner Presence in. After two weeks when you can consistently experience the warm vibration of connection in your heart you will know that it has become a part of your life. Then it is only necessary to nurture this "feeling" as often as possible for several more weeks until you can consciously move in and out of your shimmering Inner Presence with ease.

"Experience the Peaceful Love Meditation

Begin to imagine what love feels like, feeling it inside your heart. Because you have all experienced the emotion of love in your lives you know what it is, you know what it feels like. So now let us connect with that feeling. Close your eyes, take three really deep breaths, centering your attention behind your eyes. Begin to feel peaceful love within yourself, feel it quietly creeping into your body, warming your heart, and bringing a little smile to your face. Feel love pulsing in your heart with no expectations, just the feeling of love, love for yourself, love for someone else, love for God. Simply relax and feel love's sweetness flow through your body. Remain in this glowing state, breathing the feeling of this peaceful love in and out, in and out, quieting the mind, doing nothing else, just sitting, loving.

Now bring your awareness back to the room and open your eyes. What was your experience? Did love's emotion embrace you? It may take daily practice for a week or two but you now have the key to loving yourself. Love's Presence can now be a reality in your life that you can call upon at any time—if you are faithful to its Presence.

Experience Peaceful Love Flowing Through Your Heart

Love is very personal and not experienced the same way in each person. There are many ways to access our love. Speak directly to love and it will answer you in kind. Feel love flowing through your heart in and out evenly with the beating of your heart. Begin by feeling love internally, then increasing its Presence—what it tastes like—savor its essence on your tongue, in your throat, in your heart. Let it tingle up and through your body.

Look forward to this time with the peaceful love of the Universe for all its children during the events of your day, wafting love's light and vibrations into your body. Place your hand where the center of the warmth is—your heart, your throat. Without your realization peaceful love will become a part of your system, a part of all action that you take. It is this simple—love's light is ever waiting to be brought into the field of your inner vision! Love is where you are; it is your fulcrum, your Source. Love brings you into the balance of your divinity and your human physical self. Love is creative, creating from the center outward. When love is at the helm, then God and the entire Universe are there also during the continuing trajectory of your life.

Practice Bringing this Inner Seed of Love into Your Life

You must practice bringing this new feeling into your awareness wherever you are. Eventually you will be able to call it up at will, even in groups of people. As you discover the emotion of love is indeed within yourself and you can call it forth, your life will gradually, serenely change. Bringing the feeling of love into your awareness, you will see and feel love all around you. You will treat people with more thoughtfulness and kindness and you will be more loving to yourself. Your perception of life will change as you begin to love yourself from your deepest inner-self, which is divine. All previous needs and concerns are affected as this inner glowing seed-center shines forth in new and unexpected ways. You are experiencing the Secret of the Universe—All is Love. You are experiencing the truth of it, and will, for the rest of your life."

My guides, Frieda and Valto, have written a poem about the awakening of divine love.

"YOU ARE THE BELOVED

Love lives in the hearts and minds of all.
Once awakened it will glow forth
Into each life bringing peace
And comfort and inner joy,
Moving you beyond your feelings
Of aloneness, into the light
Of all creation,
Boundless in its scope.

Move beyond yourselves now
Unafraid to discover who
You truly are,
A divine child of God's love.
Unafraid to find that
Still-point-center again where
You know that love is, All That Is.

Stretch your wings, light your
Heart's fires soaring in your mind
To new heights of ecstasy.
Seek no companions
On your journey,
For you and you alone
Are the beloved."

The Experience of Connection and Inner Presence

The Feeling

You will know—when there is a feeling of "inner knowing," The awareness of a loving Presence that is constantly available. There is also a feeling of tiny fast vibrations that are slightly warm and bring a feeling of great happiness and inner peace.

You will know—when your view of events and relationships begins to change because they will be viewed with the new understanding that everyone and everything is interconnected and must be treated with equality and loving kindness. As a result there is more respect and honor for all others and the planet.

You will know—when you never feel alone again. Within you now lives a loving dependable friend and divine partner who will always support you without judgment whenever you go within your divine self for communion. Staying connected, directly and peripherally daily is essential.

> "The Description of Connection to the Universe
> Love is flowing in from your total connection to God and the Universe and it is flowing out into the environment for its replenishment as well. You drink in your loving sustenance, it resonates within your body and it uplifts your experience of that moment and the many hours after if the inspiration of your connection continues to flourish. The feeling is one of a marriage between two partners who love each other deeply. It is the deepest kind of love—felt in the deepest reaches of the body. The divine and the human magnetically radiate perfect loving energy back and forth in a magnificent symbiotic relationship."

The Experience of Inner Presence

> It is a special frequency, the God frequency, where all is made clear to you in an instant.
> It is a place of clear seeing that is transcendent and pure from the heart of the Universe itself.
> It is the feeling of rising above your normal perception of life into a higher level of true knowing.
> It is another higher level of inner awareness that can be turned on like an electric switch when accessed by contemplation on the emotion of pure love.

It is true clear inner seeing that is ever available within each person and it can be accessed through the emotion of pure love.

It is a place of clear insight into what is true.

It is a shining light that shows what is truly real, beyond what appears to be your reality at the human level.

The feeling is one of being complete; there is beauty everywhere, an inner sweetness and total comfort.

There is no strife or need for striving. Everything is perfect just as it is.

There is an inner knowingness that you are loved, you are nurtured and there is no judgment. You become aware that you have the freedom to become all that you choose, within the guidelines of the golden principles that are your road map as you partner with your soul of Inner Presence onward through life.

"The Description of this Universe of Love

Love is ever present in the Universe as energy that continues to expand outward, creating ever more energy as it moves. We see it circling over and above all the people you are trying to reach with the knowledge within this book. Give what you have found and the circling energies of Universal love will descend into hearts and minds without interference. The process is one of opening to receive on a level that is easily accessed. The energy of love is really what you will experience coming home. Home is boundless love without the body, floating free of all care and sorrow into God's embrace. Returning to the love that you don't remember as a people is of great magnitude in the greater Universe. Let each person who reads this message know that love's light is shining through these pages and directly into their hearts.

Pure Love and the Soul

The purity of love was given to you at birth. To find it again go through your normal inner-self into the light of your soul's Inner Presence. The light in your soul holds the *knowledge of pure un-bounding love. The soul of each person holds the key to awakening the purity of love for the self and all else. Once awakened this love can manifest in increasing waves of light outward from the individual, forever transforming the individual's view of the self and the world. It is never lost when the path has been found.*

The center of your being is your immortal soul of Inner Presence. It can be accessed from within when you look beyond your present knowledge. Inner presence is another name for the essence of your soul that glows or diminishes as you move from one life to another. Your Inner Presence and your soul are one and the same.

How to Access the Soul's Inner Presence
Shut the eyes, breath universal life energy in and out fully at least three times.
Let the feeling of pure love sweep through your heart and body. Feel the sweetness of love swell into a little smile on your face. Experience this transcendent feeling of inner love for a while. Make requests for yourself and others if you wish.
Thank the Universe for this precious time together.
When ready to return, open your eyes, knowing that waves of love and light continue to expand outward from your body to refresh and renew yourself and all those you come in contact with."

My Peaceful Love Meditation

Before I sit down for meditation I consciously open to the "feeling" and "inner knowing" that I am "connected." These feelings just flow over and through like a quiet wave of peace that seems to unify me with the entire cosmos. There is no division. I then sit down, close my eyes and take three deep inhalations of breath, letting my shoulders drop and look back inwardly behind my eyes. I continue to feel peaceful love within, feeling it quietly creeping throughout my body, warming my heart, and bringing a little smile to my lips. I feel it pulsing in my heart with no expectations, just the feeling of love, love for God, love for myself, love for my children and all others, love for an animal, total unification with all else. I simply relax and feel loves peaceful sweetness flow through my body. During this silent time of living within, there is the greatest feeling of gratitude, an almost overwhelming thankfulness for this gift of the amazing depth of my internal life. Sometimes during the session I ask for guidance, or to be shown what is to be done, or healing for others or myself. Often it is enough to just be there with no thoughts because I now know that by going within like this, placing myself in the hands of my divine Source, that all is taken care of without interference on my part.

When I somehow decide to return, it is slowly with eyes still shut, beginning to feel the room around me, the weather outside, the time of day. Gradually opening my eyes everything is a little misty, a time of settling back into the real world. I have been in a different place, maybe for only fifteen or twenty minutes. Afterwards I am usually able to keep this feeling of connectedness throughout the day, sometimes in a very conscious way and at other times, when in a group or teaching or painting, there is just a quiet connection. But at any time I know that I can reach inward and turn it on fully. My gratitude for this gift is boundless.

Individual Awakening Stories

"I knew early in my adulthood that I had a spiritual soundtrack running through my head, something that I did not address then because I didn't understand it. Later it became louder, as though someone was requesting my attention, and I began a process of learning from many different authors. The result was that I acknowledged a Creator, a Source, the Universe, and decided to live my life in as joyful a form as possible. Then I had an amazing experience one day in my garden. Looking up into the canopy of my Japanese maple trees, I took a deep breath of appreciation for the beautiful day, and received a direct and unmistakable jolt of joy. I knew God was reaching out and I didn't want the moment to end. It seemed that I didn't need to breathe; I was suspended in time, my mind and soul literally bursting with the feeling of love and happiness. It was clear to me that I had received a gift. I have learned to harness that feeling and can recapture it anywhere in moments of quiet reflection, having the very same experience all over again. It is always secretly within my heart, a beautiful internal symphony with no end."

Jackie, October 2011

"All that summer I had worked in a sort of animal content. I was plowing in my upper field and it was a soft afternoon with the earth turning up moist and fragrant, walking the furrows all day long, driving with peculiar care to save the horses. With such simple details of the work at hand I had found it my joy to occupy my mind. Up to that moment the most important things in the world had seemed a straight furrow and well-turned corners.

I cannot well describe it, save by the analogy of an opening door somewhere within the house of my consciousness. I had been in the dark; I seemed to emerge. I had been bound down; I seemed to leap up—and with a marvelous sudden sense of freedom and joy I stopped there in my field and looked up. And it was as if I had never looked up before. I discovered another world. It had been there before, for long and long, but I had never seen or felt it. All discoveries are made in that way; a man finds the new thing, not in nature but in himself. It was as though, concerned with plan and harness and furrow, I had never known that the world had height or color or sweet sounds, or that there was feeling in a hillside. I forgot myself or where I was. I stood a long time motionless. My dominant feeling, if I can express it, was of a strange new friendliness, a warmth, as though these hills, this field about me, the woods, had suddenly spoken to me and caressed me. It was as though I had been accepted in membership, as though I was now recognized, after long trial, as belonging here."

David Grayson, 1870-1940, United States Commissioner,
from the book, The Choice is Always Ours, Adventures
of David Grayson

"I have felt connected to the Universe, which I call Nature, as far back as I can remember. When I was little one of my favorite things was to lie down in the middle of a hay field, look at the sky and the clouds through the tall grass while listening to the crickets and the birds. In those moments I felt I was in Paradise. Ever since then I have had a special connection with the Universe.

In my mid-twenties, I realized that I had the gift of recognizing my moments of happiness. These are usually connected with Nature and my place in it. It can be on a hiking trail or simply driving along or sitting at home. The Universe talks to me. On the trails I see and enjoy every blade of grass, every pebble, every flower and the combination of all these things is a gift. These are instances of pure happiness when I feel completely connected to Nature and to my surroundings. I am filled with a joy so total that I feel like singing and dancing. When I encounter wildlife on the trails it is a message to me that I am accepted by the Universe and that I am where I belong.

One experience in London a few years ago left a deep impression on me. I was walking down a tree-lined road in Kew Gardens when I noticed about half a dozen birds around me. They were following me, flying from tree to tree or sauntering on the ground. When I stopped, they stopped. When I started walking again, they started again. As we all moved forward, they kept looking at me. This continued for the entire length of the avenue and the birds only parted from me when I had to leave the park.

I often have such messages from Nature. If I am down or feeling blue, a hike or a drive through an area I like always brings this inner joy and re-centers me. If I can't go there in person, all I need to do is close my eyes and imagine myself in one of those magic places and all becomes well again."

Francoise, May 2011

External Source Becomes Internal Source

Once you have experienced a feeling of inner connection with the Universe from an external source, as described in the personal stories above, it can then become your internal Source, your Inner

Presence. Once you know what it feels like deep within, you do not have to go back to that particular place or spiritual master for the connection! It is your own forever if you practice bringing it to your attention as often as possible. This care taking and safekeeping is perfectly described in these last two stanzas of the Frieda and Valto poem "*Sacred Bowl of Light.*

> *Hold this sacred light dearly in the*
> *Mind, handle it carefully, tenderly.*
> *It will guide you lovingly and*
> *Give to each of you its warmth*
> *And love in glowing gentleness.*
>
> *It is the light of inner knowledge.*
> *Used carefully it will give its glow*
> *Unto all who heed its call.*
> *Do not leave this sacred light*
> *Unattended for very long*
> *Or it will go out—without you.*

> *Description of an External Source for Connection*
> *The remembrance of belonging to something, if triggered,*
> *will always be a wellspring of nurture for that person.*
> *That wellspring may be tied to a holy person, a particular*
> *meadow, a tree, to nature, or an animal, etc. For you it is*
> *your heart. The finding of this nurturing place is the most*
> *important. It is never lost, even when seemingly dormant*
> *for awhile.*"

Meditation

As you continue to go within for connection with your divine Inner Presence through meditation, you can also explore using this inner state for cleansing, healing, increased happiness, a feeling of well being, and freeing the self from the body for awhile. Healing depression may take some time but your loving inner Source will show the way to bring back your equilibrium and inner light. When quiet meditation with your eyes shut has become easy, you can actively live this meditative state with your eyes open to enjoy the beauty of the world. Several creative quiet mediations with eyes closed are described below, as well as a variety of living meditations with eyes open. Living meditation can change the way you perceive the world as it opens your inner eyes to new ways of experiencing even a simple walk. Create more of your own meditations.

"Description of Meditation

Meditation is a process to reach far beyond yourself for knowledge that is unavailable in your normal state. You may look inside the self, or far off into space for inspiration, it doesn't matter. There is a divine living Presence in all things. Divine energy lives within the body, God lives within the body. As you awaken your heart to the awareness of the loving, protecting, guiding energies in your solar system, you emerge into the light of newborn understanding. Your life and the world around you are revealed to be much more than you as a people have always accepted as reality. In meditation you make the choice to awaken yourself to the love of the Universe that bonds with your psyche and soul to create enrichment in every area of your life. During this process you are creating a partnership that is as beautiful and permanent as a human relationship.

Meditation is inspiration at another level of understanding. You begin with yourself, alone, to bring yourself to a state where you feel connected to your Inner Presence. Names do not have to be given for access because the light of the soul already knows the way. Begin to learn to create with the soul's light. Meditation is a building process that brings you closer to a new reality.

The Meditation Process

We will now give you more building blocks for connection. Relax and sit or lie down comfortably, eyes closed. Focus on the light and colors under your eyelids and let us do the work. As thoughts come let them be, let them pass through and breathe in our Universal life energy deeply, in and out. Let the void speak to you in silence, radiating outward your inner heart-warmth. The warmth of the heart speaks to us in glowing colors. Hear our guidance or ask for our guidance if you wish, it is not necessary. Do not feel you need to do anything, just sit there and let us cleanse with insight and purity, because ours is the light of the world shining into you, never receding. Hold the tranquil feeling of your meditation as long as possible during your day, now that you are refreshed and totally released from care."

My Meditation Thoughts

As you begin sitting in the silence of meditation you will find that after each session, and often many days later, little bursts of inspiration or intuition will begin to flick through your mind, synchronistic events will occur and new types of information will begin to float in and out of your consciousness. As you listen and document your findings you will receive life-altering results that will, at times, amaze you.

Years ago when I was given my inner gift of love from the Universe I intuitively knew that meditation was the only way to keep it alive, so I made it an almost daily ritual of morning and nighttime heart-warmth energy meditations, including requests for guidance. Often I now awaken at 5:00 am and while lying in bed just fall into meditation. Afterwards new thoughts and ideas seem to percolate upwards as I eagerly hop out of bed to begin my day. Often during the day, for inner peace or the need to be with my Inner Presence, I sit quietly for maybe ten-minute periods while breathing deeply and spreading feelings of heart-warmth energy in and out to the world.

You will definitely experience sessions when your inner attunement during meditation seems to have evaporated. You may be trying too hard or there is just enough stress in your life to block the energy. At such times, simply sit in meditation for a while with no expectations, or stop entirely, take a walk, glorying in the natural beauty all around, and relax. The next time, you will find that "the peace beyond all understanding" will descend and all will be well again. Exploring your inner-self with the following meditations will also open you further and further to the wonders that lie within.

Quiet Meditations

Cleansing and Healing Meditation

Create in your imagination a fresh, rippling mountain stream that is just now making its way from the snows of winter, through the bright green forests and into the springtime meadows of your heart. It is a beautiful, sparkling stream with the sun shining on its smoothly running water that quietly drifts over tinkling little stones lying beneath. Listen to the water and the tinkling of the stones. Relax, enjoy, and then come back refreshed.

Healing Meditation

Use your hands to focus divine healing energy on or into the parts of your body that need special attention.

- Close your eyes and connect with inner love. Place your hand or hands on any areas that need healing. Ask for heat to be directed into your hands to focus the healing energy. If you cannot lay your hands directly on the affected part, place your hands on your heart and ask it to direct healing energy wherever it should be sent.
- Feel energy flowing into your hands, directing them to become warm. Continue to direct this energy until you feel your hands transmitting love and healing directly into the areas of your body that are affected. Stay with this healing energy until you feel a lessening of the flow, then relax and remove your hands.
- Thank God and the Universe for the healing, knowing that the work is being accomplished as you speak.
- When you have completed this process, stand up and with your hands held slightly away from the body, brush the negative energy out and away, beginning at your head

and ending at your feet. Do this at least three times always shaking your hands vigorously near your feet to get rid of the excess negative energy.

- Afterwards you will immediately feel a soothing, refreshing comfort entering both your body and your mind. You may wish to lie down for a while letting love play around in your heart for a while. It would be a good idea to have a glass of water and to take a short nap letting God and the Universe continue the healing without interference.

Happiness Meditation

Begin your morning with happiness! The happiness meditation is challenging because it tells you what your moods are! When you have a few free moments, wherever you are, give yourself this gift of happiness. We forget that we often stay in neutral all day!

- Smile! You are happy just to be happy! No special reason.
- Close or keep your eyes open and simply relax into happiness. Breathe deeply as many times as you wish, fanning warm energy all around and through your heart.
- You are beginning to feel absolutely wonderful, refreshed, and peacefully joyous.
- Relax for a while and enjoy your happy self. You may be laughing by now!
- Choose one of the following visualizations:
    * Imagine your entire body being slowly massaged in a completely nurturing way, beginning with your feet and moving upward. Let time just pass you by.
    * Let people, your family, your partner, tell you how special you are and what each one loves and appreciates about you.
    * Praise yourself for all your accomplishments, no matter how large or small they may seem to you.

- Thank the Universe for what you have received. Know that for the rest of the day you have created more happiness for yourself and those around you.

Open to Receive Meditation

How often are we really self-indulgent with ourselves? How often do we allow ourselves to receive, openly and willingly? How often do we truly appreciate ourselves? This is your time to be totally selfish and ask for anything you want. Once you bring your desires into the open you have created the possibility for success. Close your eyes, relax, welcome love into your heart and establish your connection to God and the Universe.

- Relax further and further, opening your heart and mind to receiving.
- Ask for whatever it is you would like to receive, whether it is happiness, or healing or a special gift or a problem resolution or a visit from a loved one.
- Now that you have asked you will first receive it through your imagination and visualization. See yourself in the exact scenario that you wish for. See the images and setting in your mind, living that experience as completely as you can. Live every bit of the beauty you want to receive, with no questioning, sadness or regret.
- You have now received inwardly what you asked for! You have proved that you can be self-indulgent and you can have what you want in your imagination. What you have begun is a very powerful process because thoughts do become things! We are constantly creating from intuition and thought and you have begun the process.
- Believe! Daily affirm that what you have asked for will materialize in the form of your best good, knowing that the loving Universe continually participates to bring what you choose!

Flying Meditation

When you can't sleep, or just for fun, you can practice flying while lying comfortably in bed. Send your imagination way up into the air to be free for a while. Moving off and away from earth lets you live in total freedom without worldly care until you choose to mentally return.

Close your eyes, breathe deeply, bring the warmth of love into your heart and let it spread throughout your entire body. Imagine yourself lifting off from where ever you are into the brilliance of the blue sky. Fly around for as long as you wish, horizontal with arms outstretched or vertical, arms pumping and soaring straight up. Play and tumble in the air currents, joyously free without any constraints. Laugh, sing, hum, fly with the birds, skim the mountaintops, soar over sparkling lakes and the vastness of oceans. Feel the soft smooth air flowing by, heat from the sun filling your body.

As you fly along look down at the natural beauty of your planet far below. If you get tired, climb on a cloud for a rest, falling back into its fluffy softness and disappear for as long as you wish. No need to do or think anything. Just lay there held in the arms of your billowy cloud. Perhaps you could even ride along on top of it later as it scuds across the sky. When you feel you are ready, come back to earth feeling refreshed and replenished, with new eyes to see the contents of your intimate earth world. Thank your imagination and the Universe for this ability to move out, out and away so easily. Set yourself free anytime to explore inner flying where all boundaries simply disappear.

Heal a Broken Heart Meditation

- Hold something from nature in your hands, such as—a smooth stone, crystal, flower or seedpod.
- Open your peaceful heart Inner Presence and breathe fully three times.
- Empathically feel into the object in your hand, let its qualities flow through your body.
- Experience a cleansing healing rippling stream of water flow through your body.
- Now feeling relaxed and comforted say into your heart whatever comes up for you, or whatever needs to be said.
- Ask for healing and clearing and know that it is underway.
- Stay within the quiet calm of your meditation for a while.
- When you are ready come back to normal consciousness.
- Write any insights you may have received knowing that your healing is underway.

Continue until your healing is complete, possibly adding the flying meditation to float off the earth for a while, particularly at night if sleep is difficult.

Living Meditations

Rejuvenation and Renewal Meditation

Listen to the needs of your body. It may call out for dancing or stretching, walking or jogging, crying until your heart melts or laughing loudly or screaming with the anguish. So answer its needs and give yourself at least a half hour or more to listen to the wisdom of your body that is requesting your personal attention for rejuvenation and renewal.

- Before you begin, relax into yourself until you feel the pulse of your spiritual connection through your breath and warmth in your heart.
- Take a walk, hike, jog, or drive the car on errands, dance or yell—whatever feels good to you.
- While you are moving or even driving, incorporate whatever you choose to express—joy, freedom, renewal, love, fun, anger, jealousy, and upset-ness. Live the experience vibrantly. Be as judgmental as you wish! Let it all out!
- Continue to be with what you are feeling until you experience an inner subtle release. Then let everything comfortably smooth out, keeping all the good and letting go of all the rest—let it just flow away.
- Allow your mind to casually drift over anything that is left over and ask for guidance. It may come now, or at another time, but stay open to receive and release all attachment to the outcome.
- Thank the Universe and thank yourself for giving yourself this gift. Know that what you have just created will manifest within your daily life, then completely relax and enjoy the rest of your day.

Six Senses Meditation

This is a walking meditation possibly on a busy city street.

- Begin by experiencing each one of your five physical senses separately—sight, touch, hearing, smell and taste. Choose one of the five senses as the theme for your walk and choose intuition, your sixth inner sense, as your companion.
- Create your connection to spirit or the love of the Universe and ask for guidance or make a special request.
- On your walk experience the specific sense you have chosen as exclusively as possible. Experiment with it for at least fifteen minutes, and then change to another.
- Use your intuition to pick out an object of some sort as a physical reminder of your trip.
- Thank the Universe for its guidance and document your experience in your journal including the reason for the object you found. How aware were you of your intuitive sixth sense? Was it helpful in any way? How easy was it to focus on one sense at a time? What did you learn? What was most important? Which one of your six senses would you choose to create with the next time?

Documenting the Presence

Immediately after meditation there is sometimes an almost palpable inner glowing connection that exists for a few minutes, an hour, or all day. The room and the outside world may appear brighter, softer, and even more luminous. You may find yourself smiling, content and at peace, even joyfully inspired; aware there has been a subtle shift upward, removing you from the normal need for control over all the aspects of your life. I call it documenting the Presence. This idea to describe the experience came to me one morning after a particularly inspiring meditation. I sat at my desk with paper and pencil poised, relaxed into the feeling of an inner reverie and just let the words fall into place on the paper.

The Universe Speaks

Love is the Heart of the Universe

Connection

"Connection and Choices

> *You were born with a permanent connection to the divine Universe. Each and every one of you has access to its vast knowledge and guidance. For those of you desiring to open to the fullness of your spiritual potential, the spell of this exquisite connection to your home can be bliss itself in an instant of awareness. As your desire for connection to your Source deepens, it creates the growth that may manifest finally into a reversal of balance, where the divine experience is greater than the physical presence. Each of you has the capacity for this if you choose but it is not a requirement. Remember, there is no judgment in the Universe. You absolutely make your own choices both before and after birth.*

Intense Awakening

> *When the intensity of our love is delivered to the body, it glows within the head and behind the eyes. The heart and the whole body are warmed, giving off electrical sparks of energy that penetrate every organ, bone and cell. The entire body is illuminated during this time of communion with spirit.*

Awaken to New Inner Truths

> *Your world is filled with conflicting stories about the nature of a Creator and the individual's role in a Universe that is so unknowable. Only when you come openly to us from your inner-self will you find the answers you are seeking.*

In your heart of hearts you will know! This is why each of you individually must awaken your hidden core-self to search for the essence of your existence. When reaching to discover this core level you open to a place within where your present reality subtly shifts to an awakening of new inner truths.

Who You Truly Are

You must continually go within for the search to discover who you truly are, a divine being. Daily as you build your relationship with All That Is, every fiber of your being will become attuned to the rising of your individual essence into the all-encompassing wholeness of this vast Universe. There are many ways to enter your inner world that immediately links you to the greater Universe of all knowledge. Just sitting for a while, eyes closed to the outside world, relaxing into the void lovingly is enough for a while, even ten minutes of your precious earth-time. Stopping occasionally in your numerous activities to mentally leave your body for a while continues to open the way to greater access. The more you open lovingly with no hidden agenda, the more you will begin to know more of who you truly are. And the more you trust that you are truly a part of a colossal divine complex of perfect beauty and light—the more knowledge you will be given."

A poem by Frieda and Valto

"THE PROMISE

Open, open to this Universe of love!
Open to the warmth that surrounds you
In waves of electric light.
Thrill to the ecstasy of angels,
Healing, advising and caring for you.

The heart that knows this love
Is the heart most ready
To capture the essence of God's
Invisible radiance.
Glow with this light, steady your flame
Then beam it out to the world
Out to each and everyone.

We come to heal the world,
To open people to their
Inner possibilities.
We give to each of you a part
Of ourselves and hope you hear
As your lives progress,
Forever unfolding.

Now center yourselves in the glow
Of God's love for all mankind
Each precious day.
Heed our teachings,
Love us utterly,
For we are here for all—always."

Meditation

"Release the Mind
    Floating in spacious nothingness during meditation
refreshes and replenishes the soul. You each need the

feeding of this nothingness of Universal life energy that constantly lives within and surrounds everything on planet earth. The release of your mind to allow for contact fuels every part of your body for increased aliveness. We are ever available but the mind must be short-circuited to become more creative, more knowledgeable, more intutive and more psychic. Go deeper, go higher, be swept away for a while each day if possible for the new discoveries that are waiting within. Remove the blocks and open to knowledge that is not available with the mind alone.

Breath Purifies

The breath is necessary for life, coming as it does from your Source. Everything breathes in its own way absorbing molecules of energy that float throughout your planet for sustenance of all living creatures and non-living objects. It is indeed the life and breath of the Creator, so as you breathe in this life-giving energy it can purify the inner body as well as energize it. Use the breath as a means of meditation as it will calm your circuitry, making it more adaptable to this flow of energy that is also electric. It is Universal life energy bringing us to you. Breathe calmly and comfortably, in and out, deeply, in and out, and we are there.

Empathic Meditation

To be fully present in the moment means to be consciously and lovingly aware that divinity resides in each and every human, animal and object. If you take the time to quietly be with objects or plants, you will feel their subtle essence. Just go into a type of daydream, half closing your eyes, and relax into feeling a relationship with what is around you. In this quiet relaxed state stroke your table, a book, your computer, or your clothing, feeling any subtle energy moving into your hands. In your garden stroke a flower, smell its fragrance, sniff the air. Feel a rock, stroke its surface, imagine its history, think about these things and let them stir your inner being. Stay awhile with what is surrounding you and what is stirring in your core-self. Being lovingly present in each moment with the divinity of God brings you closer to a oneness with your Creator where things great and small have equal value.

Avatars of Spirituality
You do not need to live in a state of perpetual veneration or meditation, in fact to do so creates an unbalance in the physical system and the community where sharing of goods and services creates balanced human societies. When in the company of great avatars of spirituality, transference of vibrations from the Universal field of love's energy can be given off by touch or blessing and this is a great benefit."

Document in Your Journal

What is your experience with meditation? Has it become a part of your life? Have you experimented with the different ways to experience living meditation during your normal day's activities? I hope you give yourself the pleasure of writing immediately after some of these inner sessions by Documenting the Presence. Your journal is the private place where you can store your thoughts and read them for years to come when you may very much need what you have written.

CHAPTER FOUR

INTUITIVE LISTENING WITHIN

Discover Your Inner Voices

Frieda and Valto speak: *"When life is moving smoothly along there seems to be no need for introspection because all is right in the world. The need for listening within for our guidance is still necessary for continuing peace and harmony because we expand your health and goals, helping them advance in ways that you personally might never have considered. As you link to us your life surges ahead, moving along pathways of new discoveries. Balance is the key, always balancing the opposite forces within and without. Use both intuition and listening within for guidance everyday for total accomplishment."*

This fourth key provides the way to hear intuitively the many guiding voices within that are willing teachers and helpers who will advise on many topics, assist with healing the body, provide continuing guidance, and suggest answers to help move your life to new higher levels. Begin listening directly to your voices, or begin listening through the feeling of Inner Presence.

In the previous chapter you experienced the awakening of your Inner Presence through the emotion of peaceful love. Now you will begin to use more of your innate intuitive abilities to listen within for inner voices that are always available for guiding and assisting. I became aware of "tiny guiding inner voices" as I was drifting off to sleep one night. At first when I tried to hear, there were barely discernable words or sentences that seemed to be drifting along somewhere inside my head, but they were definitely there! Fascinated, each night from then on I tried to understand them before they slipped away. Gradually over a period of several weeks I found if I inwardly asked to receive, then totally relaxed into a feeling of openness and acceptance, I could begin to pick up what was being whispered.

From then on if I stayed receptive the voices let me listen. Occasionally entire sentences would scroll across the inside of my forehead in brilliant greens or pinks like neon. Eventually it occurred to me to ask questions and they were usually answered. That was the turning point; so now the voices and I often have silent conversations just before drifting off to sleep. My inner voices speak:

> *"Sleep is usually a conscious choice to rest the body and mind in an unconscious state. It is a time for mending of the body and journeying within to reveal new aspects of the entity. It can be tampered with for answers to problems, for visions, for lucid dreaming, and for escape from reality. Its main purpose however, is rest for the body and mind, for it allows you to blend with the Universe, immersing your body in the caressing darkness of night. We watch and wait for light to bring you back to consciousness, knowing all is well. We do not leave, caring for you while you sleep. You can tell your readers these are words coming from the deepest recesses of your being."*

Probably the inner voices have been available all my life but I never paid attention. One day I asked if they would mind advising on the events of my day or little mundane things like finding parking places and such. They responded,

> *"Always we are here and helping. You are the one not listening."*

Since childhood we have been trained to use our minds to direct our lives. Each day we follow the dictates of the mind with no awareness there is other guidance available in the form of "a small voice or voices" that we can call upon at any time. Underneath the watchful eye of the mind and ego, unwilling to give up control, our internal voices speak continually to us throughout life as friends and confidants, through intuition, synchronistic events and the subconscious. Right now, with some practice, you can choose to directly tune into their messages. Frieda and Valto would you please give instruction on how to listen within?

> *"Inner guidance is given to all people who are willing to accept it in their lives. It is a gift of willingness to listen while trusting in the response of your inner voices and your guides who are forever with you. Stay within your cocoon of peace and harmony after bringing your Inner Presence into alignment. Your thoughts at that time are peaceful, loving and in tune with our energy. Your body is a perfect vessel—open to our overflowing grace. All those who ask receive answers for their lives. Ask, listen and you shall receive. Like anything in life there is the process of growth."*

Begin Listening at Night

Each night as you settle down to sleep, listen for a while to what your mind has to say, or to remember, then ask it kindly to rest and go to sleep. As you consistently bring the emotion of self-love more fully into your awareness in a meditative state try to separate your inner-self into a place of opening to receive, and listen beyond the familiar voice of your mind for other smaller voices that may sound very timid. Perhaps they have been waiting patiently, possibly many years, for recognition and participation in the unfolding of your life. You may not hear anything at first, but gradually as you continue this process you will begin to hear whispering voices advising in some way, often with disconnected thoughts. Whatever happens, just keep listening. Later, when you and your inner voices have developed trust, you can begin to ask questions. The answers may come in whispered words and sentences, or they may appear as lines of scrolled messages.

You can also ask for other forms of communication such as dream messages or guidance about a particular problem. Ask for whatever you wish and practice with the expectation of fulfillment. At the end of each session thank the Universe and your small voices for the friendship and advice you have been given and know that all you have requested will be acted upon and honored, but possibly in a different way.

Listen for Daily Guidance

When you have access to your inner voices at night, they can also become your daytime inner compasses and guides. Each day practice to quickly release your mind to openness, and then listen inwardly for a message. These are my simple processes: Think a thought, open to receive, then feel a response, or ask a question, open to receive and feel the response. Expect to receive the answer in the form of an inner message, a strong intuitive feeling, a hunch, a presentiment, or something synchronistic, like hearing just the right answer from a friend later or reading it in a book or newspaper. The answers you receive may be off the mark for a while but keep experimenting and trusting that your communication is growing stronger each day. You may need to practice for several weeks to prove to yourself that you can trust the information, but when you are ready you can use inner listening to help make decisions, for wise counsel, to resolve problems, set goals, plan for the future, etc.

Listen to Your Body

Visualization

When you are trying to make an important decision, try experimenting with different sensations in your body while visualizing two different options. Pretend that you have chosen one option and you are physically present in that location. If it is an office imagine yourself being a part of that specific office as perfectly as you can. Now that you see yourself in that environment are there any sensations in your body? Perhaps there is a sense of lightness in your chest or a feeling of warmth in your heart and hands? Do you feel peaceful and a sense of enthusiasm?

Now envision the other choice, being careful to imagine your physical presence in that environment as well. Can you see yourself cooperating with everyone, happy to be there? What do you notice in your body? Is there any resistance, is there any heaviness in your chest, is there a change in your breathing? Do you feel agitated, calm, relaxed or even cold? When you are finished you will know which choice to make because your inner authentic voice has spoken through the body.

Healing

You can also ask for healing advice for yourself and others. For your own external or internal injuries place your hand on the afflicted part and ask for the reason you were hurt, then ask for a healing. The whispered response is often a wake-up call to be more careful and attentive to your spiritual, mental and physical needs and occasionally there will be healing, perhaps over several days or weeks.

An Inner Listening Day

Choose a day or half day each week when you can be alone and relaxed but still involved in your daily activities. Begin with a meditation and stay within the joy of your inner voices and Presence as much as possible throughout this companionship with your inner self. If your awareness slips occasionally, purposefully but gently bring it back and continue. The feeling for me is a slightly misty feeling, almost a balancing of normal actions and internal feelings. The more you do this, even for an hour, the brighter your life will become and this "inner knowing" of your voices and Presence will become a normal part of your life. You will have moved to another level of consciousness.

Inner voices speak: *"The inner voices of the body are very real. They are in each and every part of the body, and every single one has its own function. Speak to them whenever you are in need of information. For healing, touch the parts that are of concern and ask the voices to advise ways to release the problem. Wait patiently for your intuitive feelings to arise to receive answers, and then follow the directions. Inner listening is the most basic key to health because you put your own body in charge. Experiment for a while until you are receiving valid information."*

The Universe Speaks

Love is the Heart of the Universe

"Listen to Inner Voices
You each have the capability of listening internally to the rich wisdom of your own personal intelligence. Discipline your instincts to regularly listen to our voices. Do it all with love in your hearts and joy on your lips of beauty. We give you a poem for this beautiful season.

SPRINGTIME

Come internally into perfect
Knowing that we are here,
Loving you, waiting for
Responses to our proddings.
Until you turn, we cannot appear.
The springtime of the earth
Is the flowering outward
Of inner yearnings.

Fragrance of jasmine, of roses,
Heady, sumptuous, delightful,
Lovingly glowing forth their beauty
For all to behold! Love the flowers,
Love the trees, love yourselves,
As beautiful as your gardens.
Grow in light and love, flowering into
Your own perfection.

Sit in your gardens, your natural world,
Feeling the eternal beauty of these
Exquisite forms. Watch the flowers
Turn their faces to the sun,
Revealing their abundance
To have and to hold forever.
Do your internal work daily
Turning always to us for knowledge.

If each of you will do this lovingly
You will find our gifts appearing
In your lives, blossoming, friendly,
Joyous, giving you peace
In times of strife! Giving you
Guidance from the center
Of your own unique being."

Document in Your Journal

You may have lots to record about your inner conversations with your guiding voices. Perhaps you have not internally heard whispered voices but you are more trusting of your intuition and an increasing number of synchronistic events are occurring in your life. I have found when communicating consistently with my inner voices, and staying within the feeling of Inner Presence, that sentences in newspaper articles, or something someone says seems to fit perfectly into what I need to know, or new opportunities and directions just open up, seemingly by magic. Inner voices, Inner Presence and intuition are all available whenever we take the time to learn from within our own bodies and trust that we will receive.

CHAPTER FIVE

STREAM OF CONSCIOUSNESS WRITING

Receive Messages and Higher Guidance

Frieda and Valto speak: *"We are constantly with you and ready to share the secrets of the Universe with anyone willing to set aside the human self long enough to let the spiritual divine self shine forth. Set your spirits afloat as you set time aside to move into our frequency of Universal energy and intelligence. Writing is easy then as you let your mind idly wander along with your writing tools, letting go of yourself for a while, watching as the words and sentences form and flow."*

This fifth key activates your intuitive abilities more deeply to clearly hear messages from the consciousness of the Universe internally (clairaudience). This vast field of knowledge can be found when the mind rests and the inner spirit surges forth during stream of consciousness writing.

Through the awakening of Inner Presence and listening within for inner voices, you are now ready for the extraordinary semi-meditative process of Stream of Consciousness Writing. When receiving messages from the Universe in this way I have always felt that the whispered words came from outside myself, but during inner listening the voices feel as if they are coming from within, so I decided to ask for answers:

> "The voices are both internal and external coming not from one or the other but both at the same time. There are many beings guiding—that is why you have difficulty naming who is speaking or directing the flow of information. It does not matter; the information comes from the Source of All for your benefit and the world. Every message is finite for the person and infinite for all. Do this practice each day until you become attuned to our messages of beauty and knowledge. You may ask specific questions and we will answer, going to greater masters if needed. We can only answer to your level of knowledge, as each of you have specific gifts that correspond to wavelengths of similar characteristics, as in radio frequencies sent between similar stations. Do you understand? There are masters available in any field, and as you move higher and higher spiritually, those answers will begin to emerge. It is in the doing that results will come."

My Stream of Consciousness Writing Experiences

When I began stream of consciousness writing I sat in meditation for at least fifteen minutes before each session. Then I would go to my desk and simply begin hand writing the first words that spilled out. At first none of the sentences made much sense, but at least I was writing effortlessly and that was what I had very much hoped would happen. Seeing sentences form, no matter what the content, kept me interested enough to keep practicing until finally I was getting complete logical statements. I did begin asking questions fairly soon because it seemed to focus the content of what was being received.

I kept all those beginning pages with any "well formed" sentences highlighted, but doing all that non-coherent writing was very tiring, with little substantive information coming forth consistently. So, without realizing it, I began half listening for repetitive sentences, stopping until the clarified thought came through. Very soon after that change I was receiving full pages that required no editing. I do still monitor punctuation but everything else is written as it was given. The writing is fun and very companionable because I am conversing with these invisible loved ones who are constantly present in my life. You will feel this companionship as well when you begin to receive answers with ease.

My process now is always the same. I sit down quietly in front of my computer for a while, but only when I am peaceful, alone and not tired, fanning the heart-warmth energy of Inner Presence up through my body. Then I simply look around slowly at all the beautiful things in my life, feeling how fortunate I am to be so at peace. I look at my home and garden, and thank the Universe for the many gifts in my life, close my eyes feeling my loving connection and write a question. Then I just sit for a few moments or minutes, waiting for the inner words to start flowing. Sometimes the sentences move off the theme a bit so I stop and dreamily focus on the question again. The writing then continues right on target, until suddenly, without any plan on my part the writing will stop or my guides will say internally that they are finished, or if it is evening they will tell me I am tired and to go to bed. This is the only way I know when this most unusual conversation is finished.

How to Receive Messages

Brief Overview of the Process

Stream of consciousness writing must always begin with a short period of meditation or a quieting of the body and mind for inner attunement with spirit. Then ask for guidance, or ask a question internally or in writing, waiting patiently and trustingly for any response. Perhaps you will wait in vain at first with pencil and paper at hand or fingers waiting on the keyboard—but keep trying.

When sentences begin to appear either quickly, slowly, tangled or disjointedly, mentally step aside from the vigilance of your mind and ego and simply watch what is effortlessly being recorded. You have begun! You have received! At first you may think it is your imagination or that your mind is responding. There is no one to tell you otherwise, so I suggest you simply continue. Possibly then in a short time as you are able to let go of your desire for successful results, you will find that very useful and often amazing information is beginning to come forth.

The Complete Process

Write only when you are alone, there is plenty of time, and your mind is clear. Before you begin, sit for a short while in meditation to create an inner stillness and a feeling of disconnect from the world. This is essential for success because you must bring yourself fully into communion with the Universe to do this work. You may begin to feel as if you are in a quiet reverie, as if your mind and thoughts have just skipped out for a while. Begin to attune your consciousness to an ideal, for example—to become your personal best.

Then sit at the computer keyboard or a table with a pad or notebook and a soft pencil in your hand and write a fairly simple question. Spread your thought out to flatness where there is no resistance, like an ocean wave swept way out to sea. If writing long hand hold the pencil very loosely, practically dangling from your fingers as you relax without any expectations until you feel the need to write something. If using the computer type both questions and answers with eyes closed, if possible, to more fully connect. As any word presents itself inwardly, write it down without thinking, and then another and another, letting the words and sentences flow out unhindered by your thought.

If nothing seems to be happening you may need to repeat your question, maybe in a different form, anything to keep the writing flowing. Don't do anything that might interfere with what your hand(s) might be inclined to write! Simply let your arm and hand(s) move with no goal whatsoever. Even though you have begun with a question you must keep your mind out of the writing and let spirit sweep into your consciousness. As sentences form, possibly including strange words or gibberish, keep writing anyway, not thinking at all for at least a complete page.

Write as often as you can, and soon without realizing it you will, more often, "feel" thoughts that need to be set down. Then in a few days or a week or two you will be amazed to see original and informative essays beginning to appear. It helps to take a playful approach in the beginning so that you can let go of any demands upon yourself for performance. There is no right or wrong way! Evaluating, censoring or filtering your thoughts at any time will stop the flow. A good session is when you write freely, not when you write well.

In later sessions when you are easily receiving information that you have requested, you will find yourself monitoring punctuation and stopping fairly often even mid-sentence until just the right words emerge. This whole process is very hard to explain but I know you will find your own way as you proceed. If answers to your questions are occasionally incorrect, clear your mind and rephrase the question, maybe at another session, perhaps it was misunderstood. Quite often I find that a question in my mind has been answered, and not the one that I requested.

When you ask simple yes or no questions your guides will probably discuss each side and may never give you a final decision. Also, don't ask, "Which job should I take?" or "Which geographic direction should I go?" You will probably never be given specific directions because spirit guides seem to like to discuss things, and give their full opinions. You may also receive confusing answers if you have strong leanings politically or particular religious preferences or you are committed to a particular position on an issue. I have never been successful with questions requesting simple direct answers, but I have read where others pose their questions in this way and they state that they are successful.

How to Find a Spiritual Guide

During stream of consciousness writing you may feel that answers to your questions come from one Source and in that case you will want to ask who or what is communicating with you and if you can address this being by name. Keep your self open and expectant for an answer and you should receive one, perhaps something totally unexpected such as two guides, or several, or a "muse." Whatever your first experiences just stay quietly open to receiving, possibly even images. In my experience I have never seen images and as far as identification is concerned I find it is confusing because I don't usually even ask. Somehow it doesn't seem important, as thinking is not a part of this process. Sometimes I do know it is God, often I know it is my guides, and other times it seems as if it a special teacher or master, or maybe Universal intelligence sharing the same information with millions of people all at the same time.

> **Frieda and Valto speak:** *"When you open to your divine Inner Presence during meditation or stream of conscious writing or prayer you are drawing in many celestial beings for answers to your needs. When you have learned to open yourself through these avenues the answers will come from possibly many kinds of intelligence. However, if you ask for a spirit guide, or guides, that request will be honored. You already have your own special guides since birth, so by asking you are opening the door to knowing who they are. Always guides are ready and waiting for your call."*

Writing Suggestions

I definitely suggest that you not show your stream of consciousness writing to anyone or discuss what you are doing, particularly close friends and family, because even the tiniest hint of a negative judgment can be so off-putting that you will never write again. As you prepare questions to the Universe they do not have to be spiritual in nature. You can ask anything that interests you or you might choose subjects that you know little about. Until you become really confident in your communication with spirit you probably won't receive information outside your area of expertise.

Creative Stream of Consciousness Writing

Create a list of dialogue topics that interest you. What are your ideals that you would like to realize or emulate? Are there Universal questions you would like to have answers to? Do you need counseling for your health or psyche or your inter-personal relationships or vocational goals? Perhaps you need inspiration for a play or a book you are writing? Or perhaps you are giving a lecture and would like to plan your notes. You might ask for daily or weekly inspirational statements or paragraphs. You may wish to have interpretations of your dreams or your meditations. Asking for something you need is a powerful approach to stream of consciousness writing. You can also use these sessions as a form of prayer where you talk things over with the Universe and receive the answers in writing. The more you use this type of communication the easier it will become and the richer will be the messages. To receive clear answers the questions should be stated as simply as possible.

The Universe Speaks

Love is the Heart of the Universe

"Stream of Consciousness Writing
> *Stream of consciousness writing is a matter of staying in frequency with higher vibrations. You can then receive messages available from those entrusted with keeping you whole and healthy and full of energy for this work on earth. Spend time with us in secret repose of your body and mind, preparing the peaceful process of receiving. Everyone is connected magically with the unknown. We are at the helm, listen—we are here!*

Release the Mind

What a person thinks controls the life, for good or ill. Life is not always easy when the mind directs every action and concern, as it does not leave room for the greater view. There are other dimensions within each individual that can be accessed without thought. That is why clearing the mind with meditation and stream of conscious writing is so important to allow new information, ideas and guidance to surface.

Messages

The ability to interact with our energies at an intuitive level is available to all. Trust and openness are required to receive messages from the divine intelligence of the Universe. We offer them as gifts to all who are willing to receive.

You are Guided

During steam of consciousness writing we are beside you guiding your pencil and hands, guiding your thoughts in directions beyond yourself. You are guided even when you do not ask. Each of you hears from within your individual crystal-seed pattern that forms your destiny of higher purpose. Call upon us whenever you need answers."

Document in Your Journal

It is important to keep a separate journal for the stream of consciousness writings so they can be kept in sequential order. You will be amazed as you look back at your dialogues with the Universe at a later date, to read again what emerged from those earlier sessions. What may have appeared at first to be inconsequential, may later take on a new and important meaning. I definitely suggest waiting until after a few weeks of writing before any editing or purging. If you have been given a guide or guides you may find a personal style is developing. In whatever way your stream of consciousness session's progress, I know that you will find your own unique way. It is an amazing process!

CHAPTER SIX

THE EIGHT GOLDEN PRINCIPLES

Frieda and Valto speak: *"The principles are a means to reach each individual with guidelines for the perfect balancing of your human and divine lives on earth. Universal principles are understood in all cultures as the way to peace, serenity, happiness and prosperity. Each culture presents these basic precepts in different formats but all are primarily the same. They align the individual with the rules for right conduct and appreciation of their human nature and physical form."*

This sixth key presents the ethical guiding principles that were given to me in several dialogues during Stream of Consciousness Writing. I was told that they are the basis of all the messages and poems throughout the book. They were first mentioned as part of the Altar of Attunement that is described in The Universe Speaks section of this chapter.

The Eight Golden Principles

1. *"Live Ethically—Honor all commitments to yourself and others. Tell the truth in all things. Live within the governing standards of your society. Honor and respect all people, animals and natural forms on planet earth.*

2. *Love Yourself—Enjoy life, laugh, dance, play and love happily. Give yourself the freedom to express all that you are. Give yourself the freedom to truly enjoy your earth form.*

3. *Stay True to Yourself—Listen to your intuition. Release your inner personal gifts. Believe in your true self and honor your individuality. Each of you is totally unique in this Universe.*

4. *Attune to Inner Spirit—Regularly practice creating your highest self. Regularly practice spiritual inner attunement to deepen your connection to God. Trust God to do the work! Let Go and Let God!*

5. *Perfect the Mind—Empower your mind to succeed in achieving your highest purpose. Empower your ego to be a helpful loving partner in all your plans. Ask your ego to support you in all your undertakings—then relax knowing it will become a partner and not an adversary. Give your mind and thoughts the freedom to change direction and make new choices.*

6. *Perfect the Body—Always honor your perfect body temple and listen deeply to its messages. Let the body guide its own perfection. Give your physical body the food and exercise it needs to stay healthy in cooperation with the spirit and mind. You are a Spirit, Mind, and Body triad.*

7. *Stretch to New Levels—Constantly stretch spiritually beyond the physical self. Embrace lovingly your connection with spirit. Stay balanced and connected to both the material visible world and the invisible world of the spirit.*

8. *Trust Your Inner Guides—Your guides will watch over you through all travail. Believe in our loving Presence forever and ever. Open to our knowledge and advice. Ask with conviction and continuing faith and you shall receive. Trust in the goodness of the Universe!"*

Central Meaning of each Principle

Frieda and Valto speak: *"We will now elaborate on the central meaning of each principal. They are each very beautiful and we hope joyous for fulfillment.*

1. *Live Ethically*

   It is each person's responsibility to live ethically and to live within earth's governing rules of conduct.

   Honor: *Honoring the self is the highest priority, as it leads to all else that you create in life. Standing for honesty and truth in all dealings, honoring the self by treating it with loving kindness and going forth with integrity in all that you choose to do, is living one's life with honor.*

   Harmony: *Abiding by the governing rules of your society harms no one, creating harmony of relationship. This does not mean that one should not stand tall for one's principles of honor. It means working within the governing system to peacefully achieve internal and external change.*

   Care-take rather than subjugate: *All forms on earth are God-given and therefore require your respect and honor. Life was not given for your dominion to treat all else as objects to be used only for the increase of your pleasure or power. You humans with your superior capabilities are to care-take rather than subjugate. Life is full of opportunities for you to do this. Talk to a tree, talk to a plant, talk to and pet lovingly your dog or cat. Moving yourselves into this kind of empathy may appear to you to be unimportant, but every living and non-living thing is deserving of your personal attention and care.*

   Relationship: *Many of you who quickly walk sidewalks and forest paths without awareness have lost your sense of relationship to the natural and man-made things of this earth. Animals are your spirit partners. Love them and treat them well if domesticated. It is your responsibility to do so. If they are of the wild, let them be, to live their* lives naturally in the environment that nourishes their existence.

2. Love Yourself

The Universe finds you perfect in every aspect, carrying nothing forward that is negative or sinful into this life! You are a divine creation in a human physical body of the purest beauty. You were created from love. It is of utmost importance for the well being of your personhood that you continue this river of love flowing constantly through your system and out into the world throughout your life. Often give yourself the freedom to express this love through your talents and your vivid imagination. Let loose all that you are for love and joy to continually inhabit your mind and body. A life lived from inner love and inner joy that is freely expressed outward creates health and bounty beyond measure.

We want you to have the freedom to laugh, to love, to dance, to sing, to create whatever it is that needs to emerge into the world. In each day there is time for a smile! The seeing and feeling of the essence of a sunset, the gradual falling of golden leaves, the happy wag of a dog's tail, the pleasure of your child coming home from school. These are everyday things waiting for your smile. Yes, honor your individuality; release your inner desires, for each of you has been given special qualities that only you can truly manifest to their maximum.

3. Stay True to Yourself

By listening to your inner-self, your intuition of inner voices, you begin the process of internal knowingness. Not from the surface results of your personality and talents can you truly know the depths of who you truly are! Inner awareness arises from consistent exploration under the surface of the mind for hints of your unique hidden memories. Sometimes they do not emerge until late in life when there is the time to devote to partnership with your divine nature. At every age we ask you to honor *your individuality, using it wisely to release the gifts you have been given for this lifetime. Listen for guidance in all that you do so that every act and thought is in harmony with the divine truth and love of who you truly are; an individual with many layers of intuitive knowledge that must be delved into and gradually revealed to find true wholeness.*

4. *Attune to Inner Spirit*

Attuning to spirit is easy because it is ever-present. The spirit of creation is not mysterious, nor is it reserved for only those who consider themselves righteous. Following the moral code of the golden principles opens the mind and heart to the possibility of knowing spirit, whereas a life lived in opposition shuts down the access. The choice must be made by the entity and has nothing to do with one's beliefs, religion or education.

God-Spirit is available to all! This most beautiful relationship is one of personal connection where the energy transmitted flows back and forth creating an intimacy of inner blissful contentment that is felt and expressed on both sides equally. Love's energy expands outward into the Universe, transcending your immediate experience. These wordless loving energy exchanges link you closer and closer to your divine nature. This sweetest relationship brings balanced peace and harmony to every aspect of your being. You do not have to question or even request that God take charge. You can simply trust your partnership and let go.

5. *Perfect the Mind*

Let your powerful mind train for the highest possible rewards you personally seek to achieve. Give your mind the freedom to learn and grow forward the special talents you have been given. Ask your mind what it would like to achieve for the welfare of your total self. Empower your mind to achieve the utmost possible. Can you separate the needs of the mind and the desires of the ego? Ask each one what is most important for your success when you are quiet and relaxed. Choose the path where both are congruent. Ask the ego, which is very willful, to support these chosen goals and let it become a loving partner, rather than an adversary. Continue to go within for guidance, never afraid to move in new directions with your thoughts.

6. *Perfect the Body*

   The body is your only real permanent home on earth. The garment that you wear while you are here. How well do you treat it? The functioning and appearance of the body are all that you can change. All bodies that are fit and seem to perform perfectly still require tune-ups of regular exercise and the consumption of nutritious food for optimum performance. The health of your body often determines how perfectly your mind can function to achieve your greatest potential. A body beset with sickness and ill health is a physical and mental hindrance. So, the honoring of and listening to the messages of the body are of primary importance. You cannot escape the physical body until you leave it behind at death.

   The spirit, mind and body smoothly function together when all three parts are synchronized. Leave one part out and dysfunction begins. The need for the uplifting of the spirit part of the equation is not necessary for some people. They are normally good sensible citizens, well grounded, cheerful and motivated to earthly accomplishments. Spirit for them is already a normal part of their triad and needs no tending. Others have perfect health, built into the seed center at birth; however, all bodies need careful and regular tending. As for the beauty of a mind that seems to need no priming to fill its well of knowledge, without continual application it will wither and die. When the spirit, mind and body are cooperating perfectly, the whole system appears to function almost automatically.

7. *Stretch to New Levels*

Bring attention to your mental, physical and creative talents and let them soar. Release all information and desires that are no longer useful. In this life you are here to stretch all of your being to new levels of accomplishment. You have been given a seed-heart-center inner-map, the strength and health of your physical body, a mind from which to create and the residence of inner spirit to guide you. Un-stick yourself from anything that is destroying your finest performance. You must forgive and forget any negativity that has shadowed your growth. To do this seek those who are skilled in such release if need be. Living and growing your personal talents forward is an imperative of the golden principles.

8. *Trust Your Inner Guides*

Guidance is constantly available to all. Turn your thoughts away from the necessities of life long enough to hear the still small voice of God-Spirit revealing the truths of the Universe. Let them spill into your mind, offering wisdom and love as you move forward throughout life. Efforting is natural for acquisition of knowledge, but to receive internal guidance non-efforting is required to hear and to receive. Let loose all thought, all desire—just be lovingly in your own unclouded silence, openly waiting. Believe and you shall receive our words of succor and love. When asked, we will guide you faithfully throughout life, offering our Universal knowledge and advice. Trust in our Presence and you will be richly rewarded."

Golden Principles Self-Evaluation

Frieda and Valto speak: *"The Golden Principles will help guide your way as you proceed to awaken the parts of yourself that may require alignment and integration. You will know, after reading them very carefully and answering the* *following questions, what is needed for the full realization of your own personal highest principals and goals."*

Our cultural heritage and our life experiences have helped create the personal moral code we choose to live by and it has helped forge many of our personal beliefs, often unknowingly. The following self-evaluation will help establish what is true for you regarding the golden principles currently, and what you might want to change or develop.

Answer each of these questions with a quick spontaneous yes, no, or maybe—then evaluate your results in as few words as possible.

1. *Live Ethically—Honor all commitments to yourself and others. Tell the truth in all things. Live within the governing standards of your society. Love others, as you are to love yourself. Honor and respect all people, animals and natural forms on planet earth.*

I honor all commitments to myself and others

I tell the truth in all things

I live within the governing standards of my society

I love others in the same way I love myself

I honor and respect all people, animals and natural forms on earth

---

Evaluation

---

2. *Love Yourself—Enjoy life! Laugh, dance, play and love happily! Love your imagination and let its voice sing. Give yourselves the freedom to express your true self. Give yourself the freedom to truly enjoy your earth form.*

I enjoy life

I laugh, dance, play and love happily

I love my imagination and let its voice sing

I give myself the freedom to express my true self

I give myself the freedom to truly enjoy myself just the way I am

Evaluation

3. *Stay True to Yourself—Listen to your intuition, your inner feelings. Release your inner personal gifts. Believe in yourself. Honor your individuality. You are totally unique in this Universe.*

I listen to my intuition

I release my inner gifts

I believe in myself

I honor my individuality because I am totally unique in the Universe

Evaluation

4. *Attune to Inner Spirit—Regularly practice spiritual inner attunement deepening your connection to God. Embrace lovingly your connection with spirit. Stay balanced and connected to both the material visible world and the invisible world of the spirit. Trust God to do the work! Let Go and Let God!*

I regularly practice and embrace my deepening connection to a higher power

I stay balanced and connected to both my physical and spiritual selves

I trust my higher power to take care of all that I need

I relax knowing that I can Let Go and Let God

Evaluation

5. *Perfect the Mind—Empower your mind to succeed in achieving your highest purpose. Empower your ego to be a helpful loving partner in all your plans. Ask your ego to support you in all your undertakings, and then relax knowing it will become a partner and not an adversary. Give your mind and thoughts the freedom to change direction and make new choices.*

I empower my mind to achieve my highest purpose and goals

I empower and ask my ego to support all my plans

I free my thoughts to change direction and make new choices

Evaluation

6. *Perfect the Body—Always honor your perfect body temple and listen deeply to its messages. Give your physical body the food and exercise it needs to stay healthy in cooperation with the spirit and mind. You are a Spirit, Mind, and Body triad.*

I honor my body temple and listen to its messages

I feed and exercise my body in a healthy manner

I feel my Spirit, Mind and Body cooperating in harmony

Evaluation

7. *Stretch to New Levels—Constantly stretch spiritually beyond the physical self. Bring attention to your mental and physical talents and let them soar. Unleash your creative spirits. Release all information and desires that are no longer useful.*

I constantly stretch spiritually

___

I let my mental and physical talents soar to new heights

___

I unleash my creative spirits

___

I release all information and desires that are no longer useful

___

Evaluation

___

8. *Trust Your Inner Guides—Your guides will watch over you through all travail. Believe in our loving Presence in everyone forever, and ever. Open to our knowledge and advice. Believe and you shall receive! Trust in the Universe!*

I know my guides or a higher power watches over me

___

I have a loving personal relationship with my higher power

___

I open myself to spiritual knowledge and advice

___

I trust in the guidance of my guides and the Universe

___

Evaluation

___

The Universe Speaks

Love is the Heart of the Universe

"The Golden Principles
   Free will was given to each of you at birth. Free will is your
   natural birthright. You each have the freedom to express
   yourselves without reservation. However, the Universe is
   offering the golden principles as guidance for peaceful
   co-existence.

The Altar of Attunement
   Come now to the high altar of perfect attunement.
   Come inside this golden cubicle of iridescent knowledge
   glimmering on the walls. Shimmering and gleaming bits
   sprinkling down and around everywhere through the
   doors of golden metal and out to the winds of time and
   space. Place your beautiful thoughts here inside the spirit
   bowl to unfold ceaselessly before your eyes. Give of
   yourself completely to this beauty, this radiance, which
   will enhance your life and all those around you. The altar
   of attunement is beautifully made of shining gold and
   flashing stones wreathed in waves of colored light. The
   doors are now open—we want you to have these images
   to create wondrous things. Hold the altar image in your
   mind at sleep, make it big, earth encompassing and make
   it small, loving and personal. Make your offerings, ask for
   visions. You will receive them!"

A poem by Frieda and Valto that describes the sacred bowl in the
Altar of Attunement.

"SACRED BOWL OF LIGHT

The sacred bowl of light is nurtured
By the sun, and filled with fishes
And many forms of life all in
Golden orbs of flashing rays.
Floating single purple suns entwine
In golden pools, visualizing the mind
With new beginnings.

The purple suns find their home
Within the mind to guide and form
For each person inner lights of
Recognition, beckoning the seeker
Onward into untold beauty
And new understandings.

Hold this sacred light dearly in the
Mind, handle it carefully, tenderly.
It will guide you lovingly and
Give to each of you its warmth
And love in glowing gentleness.

It is the light of inner knowledge!
Used carefully it will give its glow
Unto all who heed its call.
Do not leave this sacred light
Unattended for very long
Or it will go out—without you!

Voices of the Altar
Attune physically to the magic of the altar you have been
given as a symbol for growth. It is there as a model for
your perfection and to delight your senses. Inner voices
call "Come unto us, we are waiting for you in this sparkling
world of richness and joy. Come unto us regularly, growing
daily in perfect attunement in line with the golden principles
of the altar. We are the path, we are the way. We hear your

many voices calling the hosts of angels surrounding us. The knowledge we are giving you will be very beneficial to mankind. What will grow from this beginning will take on a life of its own."

A poem by Frieda and Valto about Inner Joy.

"Be creative in all things staying attuned to the golden principles. Stay in that wavelength and all will be well. We will give you a short poem now on inner joy called 'Inner Euphoria.' We know most of you have experienced it.

INNER EUPHORIA

Inner euphoria is a joyous state of
Mind when you wing upward
Internally in spirals of delight.
The good warm feelings of inner
Secrets that all is well, all is perfect.
Tiny joys bursting together
Into consciousness reminding us
Of the great happiness
This earth can offer.

Trust that by letting loose
Your flights of fancy you can
Do and be anything.
Know that abundance will
Arrive magically
Inside the psyche unbidden,
When you are ready to receive."

Document in Your Journal

Whenever I read the golden principles I am amazed at the completeness of the information that is given and the beautiful way each one is expressed. Your journal is waiting for your thoughts about the principles and your evaluation of their use and application in your life.

CHAPTER SEVEN

GOD SPEAKS WITH LOVE

Dialogues with the Universe

God speaks: *"You are all equal in the sight of God, with your own particular personality, talents and visions. Therefore, no one of you is superior or inferior to the other. Each of you spends much precious time on earth in activities or pursuits that well up deep within. As you expend this time and energy to become that which you seek, a transformation occurs—and you become what you have willed. This is the law and the Universe guides and assists you in your calling."*

This seventh key lifts the veils of illusion to reveal messages of love and council directly from our Creator. We can now know with certainty that we are intended to live joyfully, with love for ourselves and for all others.

"An Inner Kingdom
In each of you lives an inner knowledge of how and why you were born. That knowledge is secreted for you to find if you are willing or interested. You are free to govern

your lives as you wish on planet earth; it is not necessary that you know more than is given with your birthright as a human being. For those of you who wish to open beyond what you know of yourselves, there is another kingdom of love and guidance that is ever available, just waiting to be lived first internally and then, as it deepens, through love's light that flows out into the world. You can open to this inner kingdom easily through the guidance of one who knows the way. We occasionally give the way to a person or persons and this we have done through our instruction for many years with the author of this book. She has the keys to unlock the secret passageway into this other inner world of light and love that will be with you throughout your lives. Yours is the choice to travel with this wisdom along your own personal path as the knowledge of our Presence unfolds easily within. You are the children of a great unfolding, holding in your many layers of knowledge the beautiful true light of your eternal soul. Now through the writings of this illuminating book you are shown the way forward into a greater destiny of yourselves, both here on earth and in the futures of your soul.

God Awaits

Encompassed within and absorbed into your being, God is your compass, your grounding, always providing. You are the love that God loves! This is God's promise that you are never to forget: no matter where you are, no matter how low or how high, God awaits you. God does not search! You have been given the freedom to find, to seek, to not, if not, it is acceptable, but God still awaits and loves you for yourself alone. You have been created in lovingness. It is your choice to be it, to feel it, to expand it, to be all that is possible of and for yourself. Be who you are!

The Universe is One, Oneness

Knowing God directly is a choice freely offered to everyone on earth equally. God is energy, matter, electricity, time, space and all unfolding knowledge. God is the formless

71

mother/father of all. There are legions of invisible beings in the Universe who act in accordance with my Universal principles. I am the fulcrum, the balance point, they are the vibrations. All your thought vibrations are pathways opening channels for communication. Remember the Universe is One, Oneness, God—or the name chosen for the deity from all of earth's spiritual inspiring's.

What is God?

The Source of all life is within you now; it always has been and always will be. Unknowable in form but knowable in mind and heart. My form is formless yet visible in all you see. My Presence is everywhere: in the singing rain, the dripping trees, the winds of warmth and cold. It is unnecessary to search for my form, so meaningful to your understanding in a world of shapes. I am formless and forming at the same time, boundless in scope. I am the light, I am the dark, I am in all and through all waiting for your call to give all that I am. You may give me a name if you wish, any name will do.

Close your eyes, ask for my Presence and I am already there, guiding and loving you forever. At birth you were given human consciousness, my living Presence in your soul, and your own free will. What you do with your human consciousness and your free will are your determination. Your life is the result of the choices you make with those two gifts. The rich resources of earth's abundance are intended to sustain you without requiring that you search for my existence. When you do search I become personal to you. I am formless. I am All There Is. I am always with you.

Know God Directly

When you pray, you pray to the seen and unseen Universe, for God is in each and every form and concept. Knowing God directly is a choice freely offered to everyone on earth equally. There are guides, angels and other beings available to each and every one of you. The electrical vibrations of the Universe create paths to these beings who may become personal if you wish.

Cultural Religious Beliefs

God is many and varied. In the western world you have been given the name God to worship, a book called the Bible, and a messiah by the name of Jesus. Other cultures have been given their own divine teaching masters, different names for their Gods, all in their form of understanding—passing on their legendary events and myths down through the centuries. Many cultures have created pantheons of Gods and Goddesses with super human attributes that were worshiped and placed before Me in stature. You have been endlessly creative in writing your own doctrines that perpetuate the myths of your various cultures that serve to separate and divide people into opposing belief systems.

Expansion of each Soul

It is the challenge for everyone on earth to go inward into the heart for knowledge of Me. The form is not important, whether it is ritual worship, meditation, chanting or prayer. As each individual is unique, is it so strange that the paths to Me are also as unique and varied? The goal is expansion of each soul but not in one standardized form.

Naming is Not Important.

Do not worry that you call me God, or Frieda or Valto, We Are All One. I assist you in the direction that you call.

No Judgment

I do not judge, I do not set limits upon you, I respond only to the greatest good that you desire for yourselves. In your core-self, the standards of right conduct in relationship to all have been impressed. You react to that information throughout life, depending upon who you uniquely are. You are the ones who judge your actions because you internally know what right action is. There are no limits, no judgments except your own for right or wrong action. Any punishment you bring upon yourself is the result of wrong action creating negative energy.

Access to our Divinity

You ask why the knowledge of your divine self was not given at birth? You believe that if this awareness was given, that each earth life would be lived in wholeness, unity and beauty. This planet is a school of knowledge. Much has been given to each of you, your magnificent minds and your physical bodies that are intended to function perfectly for a given length of time. You were not given direct knowledge of your divine selves because it was intended for you to seek and find. Then at the next level of life, after death, your divinity will be more fully expressed into complete wholeness.

Fun and Joy

God wants people to have more fun and joy. I have given many instructions, all of them valid, but I have not touched even a tiny bit on the true joy of being human! Joy is a great part of your humanness and was given to you to express with abandon. So I say, do unwind into fun and joy whenever you can. It is a grand and glorious part of your birthright. Many of your great ones have known this and have expressed it through their delightful songs, musicals, books and magic marvels in myriads of forms. Life is not intended to be so serious.

Enjoy life

Balance of both your human and divine selves is utilization of all you have been given, including the happy, joyous, creative, adventurous expressions of your uniquely special self. You are here to enjoy the bounty of your land and the love of your fellows and to move forward in your potential. You know that moderation is the key to maximum enjoyment of all things, but once in a while why not let all the stops out?

Desire to be Human

You have chosen this earth life to be free to govern yourselves as you choose. You have removed yourselves purposefully from your true wholeness; therefore, you are experiencing yourselves as separated entities—with your own desires, goals, adventures and fulfillments. You have received your desire to be human but the longing remains in each of you to return. And so you shall when you are ready! Because you have chosen in this lifetime to separate yourselves from the mother ship of all knowledge, you have developed a belief system based solely on external values. You have chosen to forget to go inward for answers, and therefore incorrectly judge all imbalances great and small by external remedies only.

Internal Guidance

You were created from the Creator with an internal plan in place to guide you through life. You were given the free will to create your life, and parents to care for your early nourishment. It is true that you have lived before, developing skills, health, beauty, knowledge and ethics that propel you far along the way as you have practiced yourself over time. The people you selected as your parents, at another level before birth, are your guides for this life.

Fulfill Your Destiny

There are no portals or bridges because there is nothing to go through or across. I am ever available and present within your being. Learn to feel my Presence and experience the wonders that I am. See auras, laugh, love each other, love yourself, dance, leap, swim, climb—do whatever you desire knowing you are fulfilling your destiny as a divine being in a human body. You have been given the golden principles as the perfect road map to live more joyfully and more productively. Let them be your constant visual guide.

Mystery of Life

> *The mystery of life is intended, until the time is right for the next step of growth beyond this plane. Events are forthcoming that will create a new ending and beginning of earth as you know it. Now earth is expanding beyond its boundaries, honing into other planes of existence where beings of extraordinary knowledge live and work. The mystery just is—to be as you are—to grow—to listen—to be all that you can be!"*

CHAPTER EIGHT

SPIRITUAL GUIDES SPEAK
WITH MESSAGES AND POEMS

Dialogues with the Universe

Frieda and Valto speak: *"We pour our wisdom into the world for the purpose of growth for all people so that the world understands the need for cooperation at all levels for the continuing life of your planet and the health and welfare of all people. We speak from the truth of our knowledge gathered through the eons. Ours is the knowledge of wholeness, of oneness, that both earth and its people fit together in unity and peace. Our messages, our teachings, our poems are meant to deliver information outside your human abilities."*

This eighth key provides the opportunity to read the many inspirational messages and poems from my spiritual guides, Frieda and Valto. They, and many other guides and teachers, are all constantly available to be of assistance and companionship.

"Guides Names

We are known by letters of the alphabet unknown to you before. Our names are Frieda and Valto. We live otherly beside you, guiding each and every one.

Breath of Love

"We walk with you and talk with you guiding internally, but we are outside also coming from other realms far away from yours. Ours is a world of great beauty, the beauty you feel in your heart during meditations. You feel our breath of love as it vibrates through your body, never ceasing. Keep expressing it in and glowing it outward. Creating for everyone on planet earth a way to be in the vibrating center of love. Breathe it in, breathe it out. Create your new lives on earth from within its brilliant flame.

Guides Descriptions

We are guiding angels. We hover over you with wings unfolding, holding and sheltering you when called. Our petaled water caps are for protection from particles in the Universe that are wet like water. They are peaked and ruffled like sea urchins combined with seaweed, beautifully made and forming closely in silken undulating folds. We are very, very tall and thin, with soft feathery tall wings that are tucked tight to our bodies when not in flight. Our bodies are covered with luminous golden petals. Our hands are like yours, you can feel our touch. There is an aura of light surrounding us, glowing both in the dark and the light, filling the world with our messages of insight. We smile, we laugh in glee and joy. We are sometimes pranksters really wondering why you earthlings are so very serious with no time to play. We live within the altar of higher attunement that is vast in your terms, it is another Universe.

EARTH'S PRECIOUS ENVIRONMENT

Open what is already opening
In each and every heart.
God's love now pours forth
Sweetness and joy into
Earth's precious environment.

Feel the precious air around you,
Sparkling particles airborne
In glittering space.
Love your air, love your light,
Love your night of darkening velvet sky.
They are all yours for safeguarding.

We love the earth.
You do not see it clearly
In your daily toil, for you are busy
With your lives, building cities,
Families, homes, places that protect
Shielding you from harm,
Growing you forward into bigger
Lives of self-accomplishment.

We will write a poem about our location in the Universe.

LOCATION IN THE UNIVERSE

The night is long and all about us
Holding forth its dark silence
To the world in the softness
Of its shielding forms, focusing
On each and every one.
The softness of its velvet cloak,
Overspreading serenity from
The depths of Universal love.

Our location in the Universe is above
And beyond and inside
Each and every one.
We are mindful of the part
We play in your lives, not afraid to speak
When called, comforting those
Who call plaintively in the night.

We see without your knowing,
The world ever prospering to your touch,
Loving you, waiting for your call.
Awake—be glad in your home away
From home, your cradle of satisfaction,
The place where you are safe.

We see a fair and gratified world
Coming into being, here and
Sooner than you think.
Our location is one of splendor
And might where we move against
The dark forces that govern
Hosts of black angels bent on plight.

We stoke the fires, smiting
Those who do you ill
In the greater Universe.
Think well of us, call upon us,
We are loving you always.
Tendering our spirit to
Each and every one.

Guides Assist

Guides become all things: Color, gems, oils, all things harmonious, always assisting each of you to find your heart perfection. We are in the flowers, we are in the trees and grass, we are in all and of all the external world, linking you to your true divine selves.

Feeling the Presence of Frieda and Valto

"You saw us with our hands on your shoulders, our wings folded around you. You felt the energy of our love and truth holding you in spell to the moment, your hands warming as the magnetic rays streamed through your body warming and healing and coordinating all its parts. Healing is there for you to use as you learn to concentrate its energy into a force that can be directed. Practice every single day coming to divine love for instruction, for centering. As in all things on earth, patience, perseverance and trust are required to move upward into absolute knowledge. The musician practices many hours a day, loving the process, improving the method. The mystic traveler does not know the exact route but practices anyway.

Spiritual Companions

We transform lives into the illumination of love that is ever present in every heart, no matter how covered over with layers of negativity built up over many years. We, your spiritual companions, will guide the opening of each person's awareness to the love that is waiting to be released. Once the conduit is open and God's Presence is accepted, you can expect to create your life anew from that center. We are with each and every one of you in your hearts and minds, assisting in this grand and beautiful transcendence of your inner spirit.

We will write about surrendering your ego to our love and caring.

SURRENDER

It is time now to begin to
Learn to recognize the
Universal flow of goodness
Ever present in all things.
The stones of the earth,
The daffodils, the dogs,
The commonplace.

Place your love and caring
In all these things.
Wait upon our words of love
And caring whispered carefully
In your ears of knowing.
Listen to our teachings.

Surrender to the tones of
Your heart.
Forever there loving you,
Waiting for your call.
We give you all your desires,
All knowledge that you crave.
Work joyfully, always believing
In your own perfection.

This is a special poem for the night, use it well.

NIGHT

The night sky is warm and dark
Stretched thin as fabric on a drum
Playing forever the march of life.
Velvet blackness lacing together
Fiery orbs of flashing lights,
Each one it's own Universe.

We from above know the night
Intimately from another time
And space, linked to earth
For years now, our own light
Beckons us home again after flight.

Night is now becoming the
Brilliance of the day.
We behold the great beauty
In each of you, forever seeking
Your way to life's mastery.

Finding your way through
Clouds of thought, forgetting you
Are one with the Universe,
Now veiled, vapored,
Bound to earth.

We will write a poem about joyfully releasing your cares unto us.

UNDOING YOURSELF TO THE UNIVERSE

Come to us little ones,
Unleash your cares, your burdens,
Your concerns, to our yielding arms
Of love and protection.

Let us explain ourselves to you.
You do not read about us in books
You do not know we travel
With you through life.
We are your master teachers
Chosen for you alone
To govern your lives on earth.

We teach, we love, we guide.
All of you know us as intuition,
The inner listening you do
When in touch with your
Innermost being.
Take heed of our teachings,
Take heed of our Presence.

Earth books of great knowledge
Do not know of our Presence
Or acknowledge us,
For we must remain hidden.
It is our mission to do so.

83

Other Realities

Everyone has the potential to explore other realities beyond their present knowledge. It takes time and effort but well worth the doing if supported by our loving guidance. Would you like a poem about this?

EXPANSION

The density of the air is filled with
Places and events unfurled
For all to know, if they are willing.
The adventurous are the only ones
Prepared to steal into the
Mysteries of the unknown
Where they may receive visions
Catching glimpses of realities gone by
Expanding beyond into Universal energy.

This is the now of expansion!
Ready the self for further knowledge!
Prepare the way for growth beyond
This level of understanding.
Make no mistake, this is real,
Moving you beyond the earth
And into the beyond with
Maximum protection.

Expand and grow!
Give of yourself this test
Of knowing deep inside,
Where all knowledge dwells.
The golden glow of love's light
Blends with the self-awakening
Energies bound inside, growing,
Glowing outward into
Visible manifestation.

Seek Attunement

It is up to each individual to become more attuned with the spiritual force of the Universe. Everyone can come to us through whatever means is comfortable for their own psyche. We are sent from above and beyond the celestial light into your Universe for the safe keeping of all those who come in joy, in plight, and love.

INNER PATHWAYS

Walk along the pathway
With an open mind and heart,
Walk this path knowing not the way,
Obstructed occasionally,
Never blocked for long.

We see you loving each other,
Loving yourselves as you should,
Our love overspread all around
And through you, to earths end.

Do not cower or fear our love,
Do not move away,
Afraid we are not real because
You cannot see or hear us.
Our task is bringing you to the
Harmony of love.

Feel our gentle touch, melting
Your resistance to yourselves.
Guiding you into our
Overspreading wings
Of greatest love and peace.

We bring you good news,
All is well, all is flowering!
You are each growing
And blossoming in your own
Perfect way.

Change

The choice is always yours to change internally or externally. It is so easy to change beliefs and actions in an instant for the betterment of your own self-made world.

CHANGE

We see you living, exploring,
Growing toward your
Inner expressive natures.
Given mastery of self
To pursue your individual
Interests and lives.
Your expression
Is needed in the world.

You must pursue your own
Personal agendas until they
No longer seem valid.
Then do not be afraid to change.
You do not know all that is
Available to you.
Change is the way to find it.

Seeing internally is the key,
Opening doors to the true self.
Trust yourselves to be alone,
To go within, to trust what is given,
Trust the silence,
Knowing it is guidance itself,
Along your personal path.

Veils

Physical death is just a lifting of all the veils at one time, to be in a vast space of the palest blue shimmering light.

LIFTING THE VEILS

When you come to us
To find your place
We care for you with
Folded wings of saving
Protection.
We guide your life,
Giving you clues
To new behaviors.

You cannot know
Your true, true self.
Veils of illusion are
Purposefully in place.
Lovingly, often secretly
We lift the veils one by
One as you are ready,
Trust us to know.

The soul's light is magnetic, drawing others with the same intensity of light.

LIGHTING YOUR SOUL

Just stop, stop doing,
Stop thinking.
Just stop for a while in
Contemplation of your
Inner divine self.

As you do this,
The spiritual Universe
Opens, gradually lighting
Your soul.

*We, your spiritual companions
Make our appearance,
Creating beauty that can
Spill over into your life,
In ever increasing frequency.*

*Meditation creates God Consciousness—the conscious awareness
that God lives within the self.*

MEDITATION

*Meditation is a way
Of opening and
Contemplating the invisible
World of your divine nature.*

*Seek its nurture, seek its solace.
Place yourself in this quiet
Place for longer and longer
Periods for the beautiful
Release of your true divinity.*

*Go inside yourselves
Daily, faithfully!
Then, see your inner selves
Becoming beautifully
And fully expressed."*

CHAPTER NINE

THE UNIVERSE SPEAKS WITH GUIDANCE

Dialogues with the Universe

The Universe speaks: *"These messages of love and guidance are filled with our heart energy. Everyone so inspired to read them will be awakened to new potential. They are a compilation of teachings about the giant pattern of the Universe where all parts are intended to fit together in perfect order. Earth's beauty and light are constantly on display in thousands of ways but the grandness of the overall plan cannot be easily seen. We offer here a more enlarged view."*

This ninth key reveals the messages of knowledge and instruction that are given directly from the spiritual Universe frequency. This vast guidance is available in all languages and dialects throughout the world for all those who choose to attune themselves to receive this wisdom.

Abundance and Sharing

"Create Abundance

You will have well-being and abundance by planning each step of the way, setting little practical goals and working toward them consistently. Begin where you are now with clarity and purpose, believing in your success, planning for your future starting right this minute, committing real time and energy. Set inner goals as well, staying tuned to our higher call of goodness.

Give to Receive

Select a course beyond your personal selves of giving to the world, no matter how small. Trust and completely know that what you give, you shall receive! It is the only way. It is the law of individual creation on your planet. Trust and give toward the good of all and good shall be returned in full measure. This is the exacting equation.

Create with Money

Money is a medium of exchange used to barter for what you wish to have or own. It is a neutral medium and a flowing commodity that to be used properly must be shared by all equally, where all have access to the common good. Money used in this way multiplies exponentially, as the fish and loaves story in your Christian Bible. We ask you to use money to increase everyone's standard of living in whatever way is possible. The law of love and the law of money are the same. The one a part of the body and soul lighting up the world, the other a medium of neutral exchange that expresses unilaterally without preference.

To deprive yourself for others is not the way. You are to manifest in this life all that has been given you to achieve. Choosing money to create with is fair and logical, as it provides the safety and welfare that is needed to create your unique and special place in the world. Choose to create with money but keep it flowing! Thinking of money as the equivalent of love will help you be fair in *your dealings with others. You do not have to give love or money to those who are unworthy. You can turn your backs on people who do not deserve your attention and good will. Choose those to whom you wish your money and love to flow for the perfection of the law, which is to create abundance.*

Ask for Money

Sit as you do in meditation and ask. There is no secret about receiving anything you wish. The Universe does not know what you desire until you ask! Put energy into your words and speak the power of your desires to receive! Wishing we hear, desires we hear. But, until the entity desires a particular outcome and places energy into receiving, the Universe does not participate. The strength of your word is required but desire alone can be so strong that the result expresses itself without the effort of creating a specific plan for achievement.

Say, speak what you desire, laugh, sing, be joyous about what you want to create, make pictures, make tangible evidence of what you truly want money to do for you. Call the flow of money to yourself diligently and faithfully, giving sincerity and praise to your requests. It will be given to you as you specify in the nature of your heart's desire. Life is constantly expressing and will do so in the direction of your choosing if you make your requests known through your creative, imaginative abilities, co-creating with the nature of creation.

Circulation of Money for Peace

Money multiplies when given to benefit others. When ill used to impact society negatively or for personal gain only, the law of money is put to disservice. It is not doing its job of creating wealth and stability for all to raise the consciousness of the entire planet. All countries large and small need to know the importance of using money for the good of all peoples on planet earth. When used in this way, money is in circulation and doing its job to increase the living standard and welfare of all economies and individuals. All the major powers recognize this need to help each other, if only to preserve their own economies and remain on friendly terms with each other for the stabilization of all.

Conservative thinkers do not realize this, and would use money to benefit only their own countries. Like a giant puzzle, all pieces need to fit together peacefully so there are none missing in the global picture puzzle. Seen this way, with all the pieces fitting together perfectly, you can see how the correct circulation of money is the only right answer for health and wealth of all globally."

The Body

"Create a Healthy Body and Mind
Be mindful of your relationships, the food and drink you place in your bodies, and your thoughts, always directed toward healthy accomplishment. When the body is weak it can suck up unhealthy ions that distribute themselves throughout the system, disrupting and breaking it down.

Heal with Loving Energy
Through the intent of the individual, healing hands and eyes can be created and enhanced. When you awaken your inner-self with the desire to heal, those special gifts are available to you. Healing the body is very simple. Rub your hands together briskly and slap them together for more circulation. Lay them on the afflicted part and relax into the sweetness of inner love. Imagine golden light spreading throughout the body from your hands. Stay quiet and relaxed for a while knowing the healing is taking place and all is well. Afterwards give thanks and accept what was given. Continue daily if necessary. The secret of healing is to feel the power of love within, then beam its energy throughout the body until the body is completely reunited in health.

Heal with Spiritual Guidance

If healing is required, seek spiritual guidance within your churches, within your community or within the reading of uplifting books. Inner peace will be achieved as you begin to realize that all beings are connected to the loving Source of all creation, and that each and every one of you who ask is guided lovingly and tenderly throughout life.

Heal with Personal Energy Fields

You can change conditions of ill health and before-birth choices through your personal energy fields directed into the opposing affliction or blockage.

Chakra Energy

Chakras exist in the body as centers of energy that can be awakened through contemplation with the mystic forces that surround in waves of light. Our healing energy affects the entire body, cleansing and opening constrictions of all types.

Ascetic Energy

The yogi creates ascetic energy that is essentially invisible but manifests in others who carry it forward.

The Etheric Aura

Each person's etheric aura has colors that are their own and can be seen by many. Ask to see auras with half closed eyes, at first in a semi-conscious state, looking first for a shadowy outline around the entire body. In semi darkness when your inner guard is down they are easier to see. Practice in the same semi-conscious state in the daytime and you will begin to see the colored bands and rays of your aura.

Healthy Aging

Healing energy is always flowing through the body, interrupting stagnant areas of blockage that are created from many sources: food, drink, the emotions, physical damage, birth defects and so on. Age coarsens and constricts the vessels as the fluids of the body begin to shut down voluntarily. As one ages, if activity is maintained and healthy foods are directed into the body, the shutting down process will be delayed—until finally there is a need for the soul to leave and go forth into a new life, holding the enrichment of an earth life that increased its light.

Sex and Ecstasy

The sexual experience may be entered into without the emotion of love; sex is then only a function of the appetites of the body. It is not essential that love be present for procreation. The sexual act between loving partners is the zenith of the emotional experience you can reach on earth. Intense ecstasy of self can be achieved without a partner if the initiate is willing to go beyond the typical life on earth. Communion with the totality of love's heart is intense and white hot but it cannot be reached at the level of normal desire. The yogis reach this state and are transported way beyond where you ever intend to go. But it is possible for all! The desire and the willingness must be there for continuous communion. Yogis have chosen this path to bring into consciousness that which is known only at the core level. You do not need to do this, nor is it important for salvation. Their life is no higher in estimation than yours. They have chosen to experience beyond the standard platform of human performance.

Addiction

Addiction is the grasping sucking form of evil incarnate. Once entrenched, the individual's power is diminished and a new reality is locked in place, seemingly as normal. Diminishment of the psyche, bodily functions, and interaction on all levels occurs and requires accomplished healers to take charge of the life so affected. If the body and mind are not brought into the light of coordination through healing, this dark or evil side may travel with the afflicted one through many life times.

Death, Birth, Health and Illness

Death is not death, as you know it, you go on living. If all earth's people would simply learn to flow into this other state of being, there would be no pain of separation. Death, or the disappearance of the body, is a cycle that you do not wish to meet, but you do not question the cycle of birth. The last is joyous, the other is saddening and often overpowering for the living who must continue. Death can be arranged. It can be invited to visit at a time of your choosing after your work life on earth is ended.

Each life is holy, divine, pure in spirit, pure in conception. Grow its purity forward throughout your life in as perfect a form as you can imagine. Keep the health of your body intact, nurture all that you have been given and fulfill your obligations to yourself and humanity. Upon completion of all that you are, you may ask for deliverance to another place in the infinite Universe and your request will be honored, provided that centering within our healing energies is consistently practiced.

You ask about early death, disease, physical and mental deformity. All is not perfect on your planet and all are not created equally fit in both mind and body. You are each given what you choose before birth, this is not for you to question.

Death is Expansion

As you pass over from this life into another you will find that your life, as you knew it on earth, was limited. The expanded view at your passing will be a part of the divine destiny you have grown into. The promise, given to all, is the expansion of your earth life at another higher level within the infinite Universe. There is no judgment from the creative force on planet earth. You are here to utilize all the physical, mental and spiritual resources available. You were also given all that is needed to become a more realized human and divine being. This life that you have magnified on earth will continue to grow in beauty and strength after death."

Inner-Self

"The Soul

The soul is the purest form of yourself, for it gives birth to all that you are. It is your task here on earth to expand its limits beyond what it knows of itself. The life of the soul is experience, lived through the body that lives through the mind and heart, creating a circle of continuing creation. Each person reflects outward its inner radiance. When it is diminished—as is possible through impoverishment, negativity of the entity, ill health, misuse of the body and poisons of all types—the soul constricts, waiting its turn to expand again in another cycle of life, not necessarily on earth.

Magnify your Soul

The soul can be fed and therefore magnified through the activities that you choose to elevate to prominence throughout your lifetime. It is the crystal-seed center of who you are, encompassing all your bodily and mental functions. As you move purposefully toward elevating and enhancing all the incredible dimensions of your being, your soul-self will rise in joy and praise. Love for yourself is love for your soul. Bring it as much light as possible through your desire to move beyond your human-ness and into the divinity of which you are a part. This sweetest and dearest friend will send its many thanks outward, lighting your way.

Definitions of the Soul

The soul is the total inner core, the crystal-seed center of yourself. It is the mastermind, the control center, establishing its mini-Universe of love and attachment to All That Is. Because the soul can grow or diminish, we call it a seed. Very understandable, is it not? So very beautiful also, because it is crystalline—crystal clear at birth and faceted, taking on many colors as you move higher and higher in your vibrations with the God Of All.

Thinking of your inner core or crystal-seed center in this way you can see how all your thoughts and actions can affect its overall beauty. Therefore, the converse would be a darkening and clouding of this many faceted jewel. May we say once again how beautiful is your crystal-seed center, your jewel. Light it with your fires, light it with your nobleness of righteous choices and bring it forth for others to see and experience!

Inner Joy

You can have more joy in your life by often taking the time to appreciate what you have been given and bringing your special attributes into fruition. Your whole life is intended to be joyous and can be even more so if you link yourself inwardly to love that is like a mothers love for all her children! The Mother Ship of all Knowledge is multi-gendered encompassing all the male and female qualities of love and caring, constantly flowing, drawing you into that embrace. For those of you who wish to transcend the human level of joy, you may choose to experience a higher level of joy and light by going within each day to commune with your Mother Ship of all Knowledge. Joy at this higher level is both exquisitely luminous and transcending. It can also perfume the air that you breathe.

The Mother Ship of All Knowledge

This is where you are from, the womb of the mother. The Universe is a great womb out of which everything is born in flashes of energy and light. It is colossal and indescribable, not a place, but a space that nurtures a complexity that is beyond description. The Mother Ship of All Knowledge is the Creator itself, genderless and ever expanding.

The Higher Self and the Subconscious

Often your teachers will instruct that your higher self is the link to your Source. Speak to your higher self in this way

97

if you wish and it will always respond. Naming and titling are totally unimportant as we receive only in wavelengths of energy, using words for your understanding only. We equate the inner-self with the subconscious that is your hidden inner knowing.

Intuition and Synchronicity

Answers and directions are formed out of the connecting electrical energy within life itself and then reformed into individual hunches, flash thoughts, feelings, teachers, encounters, articles, music, etc."

Religion

"Light of Salvation

Love is the only way to make God a reality in your life! The concept of electricity is accurate. Plug into the Universal conduit for connection. When connected, God's Universal law is available to all. Within this connection, attune your daily lives to God's vibration, living within the golden principals to further God's love throughout the world. For in each one of you is born a light of salvation that burns forever down through eternity. You are given the choice to turn it on and be in its light or to forget this privilege or to turn away knowing nothing of your true potential or to even turn so completely away that sadness and chaos are created.

Deities are All One

God, Brahma, Buddha, Allah, Jesus, are each separately identified for earth's different cultures. Guides, angels, good beings, all work together in unity. We may ask for one or all, their responses will be the same.

Heaven and Hell

Organized religions have created these so called "places" and we understand their meaning. There is no actual heaven or hell. However, you can create your own personal heaven and hell."

Two poems by Frieda and Valto.

"BIRTH

Easter begins a cycle of birth
Up through spring rain
And freshly turned
Rich, black earth.
Each tiny insignificant seed
A miracle of life
Awaiting your loving
Nourishment to flower
Into its own unique perfection.

Easter is birth, a cleansing,
A making ready for ripening
Of the soul's journey into light.

Place desires in your
Seed-heart center,
The soul of your being,
Where they glow richly into life
Tended by your constant faith,
And our overflowing love.

THE ONE CREATOR

The word of God is always with you
In every dialect and every religion.
God speaks to all in the dialect
That all can understand.

Mine is the voice of comfort in
Times of sorrow,
The voice of praise,
In times of heroics.

You are in need of learning
The world is one unit of knowledge
Not broken up into pieces
Of believers in one faith or another!

The poem Easter is meant for all.
The signifier of birth everywhere!
All life tethers to the one unifier,
The one Creator
Of so many names."

Earth

"Choice of Physical Life
You have each chosen to experience a physical life on this beautiful planet. If all struggles for survival were removed, the need to achieve peaceful co-existence would not exist. All would be perfect, each totally content with the reaping and the sowing, the care taking of the global family and your earth home. Abundance would be continually supplied in a beautifully balanced symbiotic relationship. Can you imagine living this utopian ideal?

Balance of Divine and Human Natures
Righteous choices begin with peace, harmony, love, equality, brotherhood and giving of oneself to raise the consciousness of yourself first, then your neighboring territories, then your nation, into brotherhood with all others. Bring into balance your divine and human natures. If each will strive for this model, the earth will release its bounty to provide for all.

Earth Time
Earth time is not a reality in our realm.

Earth's Operating System
The Universe is continuing to set up wavelengths of increasing frequency for greater access. Earth has a

system of its own that operates without interference at a certain speed and decibel level. Color, form, life, speech, hearing, breath, matter, cells, they are all calibrated efficiently to their own unit of energy. Each operates independently within the quantum system. As you fine-tune your human electrical frequencies, you activate responses from sympathetic systems. In other words, the organizing pattern of your Universe responds to directed thought through actual impressions into the elastic skin of the ether. Numerous harmonious messages create impacts that are sensed as large indentations.

You ask about negativity, hate, war, and tyrants. All thought penetrates! The more potent the energy the greater the indentation. The system works for good and evil, effectively demonstrating the principle of cause and effect. The greater the intent the more result. You ask where your personal relationships with God fit. The God response is immediate and ever-present. Your abilities are usually limited to gathering personal growth rather than physical change of the environment, although it is possible at intense frequencies. Your sourcing with the vast intelligence of the Universe is only limited by your lack of belief and faith.

DNA and Instinct

There is a master pattern that unfolds for all living things, according to each category of species. Each separate classification is programmed to emerge in a particular way. This is the seed pattern, which you call DNA in humans, but it resides in all organic forms on earth. The iris flower, the oak tree, the bumblebee, all forms must respond automatically to the call of their individual seed patterns. Fish, insects, birds, also respond automatically to this impulse which you call instinct. They must answer the call of their inner patterning. The animals that are cared for lovingly by their owners develop a higher patterning over time. Primates especially have developed far beyond the basic instinctive response. Loving care can bring forth newfound responses even in flowers.

The Four Basic Elements

The elements of water, earth, air, and fire are essential for life to exist. They are also the variables bringing change and chance into your system on a regular basis. The rhythm of the magnetic tides, the wind that blows or rustles or destroys, the sun that warms or burns, all are part of a vast system that gives life and takes it away. Your particular Universe is in a state of constant ebb and flow on many levels.

Earth's Pattern of Perfection

Can you not see the giant pattern of perfection that exists to take care of your every need? You are the lilies of the field, given the right to do as you wish. You human beings with your magnificent brains were given the consciousness to make choices, to create your own lives, to create masterworks with all that has been given you. God, the invisible Universe, the master plan has given you this right. The perfection is here for you to find.

The Master Plan

You can think of God as the master wizard template, as in your computer, creating perfect products from its perfect self. All organic life on this planet contains the master wizard template. Imagine all this perfection of living things existing together on planet earth in perfect harmony because the master template is stamping out only perfect images of what itself imagines. Can you picture this kind of perfection on earth? No deviation, no struggle, no change—only perfect joy and beauty. No, your planet is not cookie cutter perfect, it is an action planet full of contradictions.

The example of the computer template is given to you because, if the directions are not followed perfectly, the results can be lost in the process. The areas you fill in on the template are equivalent to your free will. These are the choices you make throughout your life. This master plan of perfection is held deep within your core-self. Each person has the awareness to recognize it and intuitively knows when there is deviation. You call this part of yourself the conscience. You are all accountable to the master plan for right action, but you have also been given the freedom to deviate. Perfection was not intended for this planet.

The Global Model

Many in all walks of life recognize and consistently work toward wholeness and freedom of choice. However, many societies globally have lost all personal power to tyranny and oppression. Over many lifetimes those clouds will gradually be lifted through peaceful settlement of major issues and new social and economic agreements. Slowly over time the good of all will become the global model.

Acts of Kindness

We ask each of you to begin the process of moving beyond the needs of the ego-self in your present thinking and future planning. We ask that you begin to shift your thoughts away from this constant desire for self-gratification and begin to offer genuine small acts of kindness to others. As you continue to perform these simple gestures you are greatly contributing to the much greater cause of health and wholeness for all. When you commit to giving something of your light to others, there will begin to be a subtle higher shift of consciousness in groups of people around the world. Offering yourselves in this way you will have rendered a great service in the reconstruction of the present self-serving paradigm. Will you do this?

Rise in Consciousness

Because earth's people are born in and live in a variety of habitats, they adapt as animals do to their terrains, food and water sources in order to survive. You must know that many peoples on your planet exist marginally, protecting fiercely their personal territory. The "world playing field" of education and access to earth's bounty is not equal. What you cannot see is the process of change that will gradually occur as more and more of the worlds peoples rise in consciousness, where all recognize their divinity and throw off their ego-directed orientation to each other and the world. In your lifetime there is advancement in soul consciousness throughout the planet. Gradually, many lifetimes from now, a destiny of perfection will be created. Those of you who are working toward this grand design, through your loving inner work, are raising strong wavelengths of positive magnetic energy throughout the planet.

Earth a School of Knowledge

Life on earth is an interaction of specific elements existing in your atmosphere that allow the creation of living matter. Your planet contains these necessary components to give birth to and sustain a myriad of interdependent forms. Yours is a learning Universe, a school of knowledge, a location in the Universe where you have the opportunity to express the electric light and love from which you were created. You have the power for this and you are requested to use it for the expansion of goodness throughout your earth home!

Animals are Spirit Partners

Animals are highly respected in our world of truth. They are caregivers, they are food, they are beasts of burden, they are for you to use with respect and love, if that is your relationship. They have their own lives apart from yours that is tied to an inner awareness of their own instinctive nature—their dog-ness, or bear-ness, or beaver-ness. They are totally one with their nature, having no ability to change or question. They love, they anger, and they fight, by instinct alone of what they are. If you live with animals treat them with loving kindness for they are your spirit partners. Look them in the eyes and you will see this. If you work with animals give them all they need for mutual benefit. All animals respond to love and care positively within their own awareness. The animals you have domesticated to work for you are dependent upon your kindly protection. You have created what you are now intended to take care of, with compassion.

Animals Souls

The human soul is familiar to you and can be grown and beautified throughout life. Animals' souls are tied to instinct where one animal is kinder or more aggressive than another. Their souls do not die therefore you will encounter them after death. All manner of species is a part of the after death experience and a part of the Mother Ship that we have spoken of before.

Inner Conflict

You all have beautiful inner beauty and you all have your base nature, the riddle you live with on earth. Each of you solves the riddle, the inner conflict, according to your inner-seed-pattern that you were born with. How much of the beauty and how much of the dark emerge in your lives depends upon your willingness (your free will) and your seed patterning. Humans believe that goodness and beauty should surmount darkness (the metaphor for evil), and so it is meant to be on your planet.

Beauty and the Beast

Yours is a magnetic and electrical Universe that responds to the laws of positive and negative vibrations and force as the balance shifts. The emergent responses are physical demonstrations of the beast let loose at the present time in certain locations on your planet into greater darkness of the soul. A goal on planet earth is to help release beauty from the beast of darkness. This duality of your planet will ever be thus until the minds and hearts of mass humanity are so directed toward inner peace and harmony that the blockages of darkness are removed. This message is intended to help show the way with the story of beauty *and the beast as a metaphor. In the work you do with your core selves you may also consider darkness to be that hidden part of yourself that invites exploration, waiting to unfold its richness. Both the darkness and the light in your lives can be beautiful.*

Opposites Train Perception

Opposites are a part of your system that affect each life. Goodness, kindness, beauty, health, love are all countered by evil, selfishness, ugliness, sickness and hate. Each opposite is in each of you, expressing itself in different quantities in response to your interior and exterior environment: psyche, soul, health, family, relationships, education, and location on the planet. Pairs of opposites train your perception to see, hear, feel and sense information: light and dark, tall and short, in and out, up and down, curved and straight, rough and smooth, elastic and rigid, wet and dry, hot and cold, open and shut, pull and push, walk and run, vertical and horizontal, black and white, soft and hard, sharp and dull. You are all a part of the opposite forces in earth's system.

Energy Focused on War

War, as you call it, is an outward manifestation of inner hatred, rebellion and anxiety of a group, tribe or nation unable to contain it. The act of war moves the inner crisis of containment outward into extreme action. This need for war will disappear only when the inner stillness of peace is obtained in fair dealings with all others, with oneself and your planet. When you are willing to share equally with each other, earth's resources, your personal bounty, your love—then individual, tribal and national prejudices will fall away, leaving each of you the quietness of spirit. War against evil can be countenanced if its ultimate benefit is parochial, truly raising all life on the planet to a higher level. Then and then only is war necessary and acceptable. The agenda for war must include an agenda for peace and equality.

When the major powers of your world interact with each other, the energy for decisions constricts into a unity that filters out any deviation from the chosen goal. Voices of moderation that should be heard are driven out by the will of those with the strongest desire for gain. Once again Universal law is proven on a grand scale. When energy is focused toward a given goal, that goal will be achieved for either good or ill. Therefore, if the greater energy is focused on the need for war, for whatever reason, there will be war. Also, without the focused intent and energy placed on raising the life of other nations on this planet, then this act will not be beneficial and will end in continuing upheaval around the world.

It is important that you contemplate these things. Life is not good on your planet for so many. You have not learned to live together peacefully, each doing your share without regard for personal gain. Your women, your animals, your poor, your environment, are used continuously for others' gain. And it must stop or you will be without a home! Life as you know it will be striven from you! The planet can only take so much abuse and defilement. Do your best to bring gladness and bounty to others, in your heart first, then out through your deeds of generosity. Each gift from the heart is a gift of loving energy for the planet.

World Cooperation

World cooperation is possible, but not in your lifetime. The paradigm of mega powers suppressing the weak is still in play and more lethal as you harness world resources to your bidding for more and more strength and power. Controlling dominance without regard for the weak, the suppressed, the underprivileged, the under-educated is emerging as the directing force. World order will be restored and global cooperation will result, but much earth-time will pass before equality and liberty for all shine forth. Begin today your focused intent on peace for the planet and safety for earth's peoples. Join the many

107

prayer groups and voice your concerns, because focused intent brings forth incredible results.

Create the Utopian World

The forces of good and evil are ever-present on your planet. The pendulum is an apt description of the cycles of these two forces as their energies fluctuate in strength and power. The dark energies will never totally eclipse the light energies because the weight of the light is greater. The worldwide manifestations of anger, revenge and hate are the direct result of focused energy directed into the force of evil. Dark forces manifest around the dark emotions. All of you whose mission it is to bring more light and creative energy into the world will gradually shift the balance to the light and create the utopian world of your aspirations."

The Universe

"Process of Creation

Creation begins with a thought, a model or a concept and expands outward into the various Universes through its vibrations of electrical energy. All that is created begins this way. The clarity of the thought or idea is the beginning, carried forward and outward from All That Is. This thought or imagining is acted upon by the magnetism of like energies bringing it outward into form or realization. First, clarity of vision for accomplishment for good or evil. Next, the action of electric magnetic knowledge drives the impulse for resolution forward into demonstrable form. This is the process of creation that each of you continues as you imagine and create.

Heaven and Nirvana

All supplication is the request for release from a measure of darkness into the goodness and sweetness of light. Were it not for this pair of opposites, all you would know is the brightness of the one or the darkness of the other.

Yes, there are worlds of perfection where the light has so prevailed that what you call heaven or nirvana is all that is experienced. Each of you can have the same experience internally in the beginning, then outwardly into your society as you flower and grow. The way to this internal bliss and harmonious joy is to release your fear, bringing our loving Presence into your hearts and trusting in our guidance. This is hard to do because your ego begins to distract you from your innermost yearnings. The soul seeks light, the heart seeks love, the body seeks sustenance, the planet seeks equilibrium, your guides seek communication, and evil seeks adherents.

The Power of Light and Dark Energies

There is a dark side in your Universe affecting to some extent all people. Protection is necessary to avoid its grasp for it has great power over what it chooses to know deeply. All are susceptible to its clinging grasp and all of you allow some of this darkness into your lives. Your world and the entire Universe of endless galaxies are filled with opposites. Dark and light are the strongest pair on your planet, always balancing off each other, striving for dominance. Choosing the light over the dark is the choice of the All in All.

Light is the Chosen Goal

Light is the chosen goal of all creation; the inner impulse toward perfection overshadows the evil opposite. Light, beauty, goodness and perfection will prevail as you move higher and higher in the understanding of your true divinity. Trust Universal intelligence to continually guide your pathway ever upward. As you each choose this guidance, love for yourselves, love for your planet, and the divine energy of the Universe—the ability of the earth to absorb what it needs will manifest.

CHAPTER TEN

TRANFORM YOUR LIFE EXPERIENCE

New Possibilities and Vistas

God speaks: "*Examine your life through Inner Presence that is now shimmering quietly inside your heart. Consider every action and experience in your life through its illumination. Let this light open into the recesses of your memory to extract what is needed to create ways to grow and open your life to new possibilities and vistas. Allow your divine Inner Presence to show the way with its inner light of compassion and understanding.*"

This tenth key unfolds the way to break free from unconscious habitual modes of reacting to life to embrace higher states of being. You will learn, through your connection to Inner Presence, new ways to move through life. In these higher states you are calling forth your higher purpose and automatically removing boundaries that you may have unintentionally set for yourself.

The primary goal in all the preceding chapters has been to provide the keys to awaken Inner Presence to interact with the loving caring Universe of love. In this chapter the central focus is on the joy of going inward to explore your present and past life experiences to re-discover more of who you truly are. To step out of your own dramas long enough to examine and remove lingering memories and thought patterns that may be hindering your progress. You will begin to realize, as you work with this material, that when both your human and divine natures are equally balanced the rewards will be expressed in all areas of your life. As you continue to bring more and more divine Presence into your daily life, your human self may begin to let you know in subtle ways that it too needs more individual attention, acceptance and understanding. The Universe would like to address physical health and wholeness.

> "Balance of all aspects is intended for completion as a human being. Your physical body is a masterpiece of utility and is intended to serve you well and faithfully throughout your sojourn on earth. Treat it well, giving it the exercise that it needs for strength and dexterity. Give it the foods that it requires for health of the tissue, bone and blood, and for the cells that create life. Because you are both of the earth, (human), and from your God-Source, (divine), yours is the responsibility to continually create at both levels of your being to make yourself whole. As you receive our light and love, new knowledge is born that directs you inward. Moving from within to access your divine self you can set up dialogues that affect all aspects of who you truly are. We honor and treasure those of you who are on this path to wholeness."

I asked how the connection of heart-warmth energy is helpful for this inner journey.

> "Linking with heart-warmth energy you will start to let go of long held judgments, anger, defensiveness, grudges, revenge, inequality, derision, sadness and self-pity. Shining love's light regularly into your body gradually illuminates this stored material, which then quietly surfaces into conscious attention for examination. You

will find yourself questioning whether you need to carry old worn-out emotions and thoughts any further, when they are getting heavier and heavier to carry. Do worn out attitudes or judgments have further value or importance in your life? Has your over-sized or under-sized ego been leading your life for too long now? All of this gradually comes forth to be seen lovingly, to then be adjusted or discarded as your truer and simpler life begins."

Your Life History Timeline

To discover the basic facts of your life history, make a chronological list of only the most important events of your life. Begin with your birth, inserting all your significant events and influences that have emotional attachments, and end with the current date and year. Take your time, writing down anything that may seem important, knowing you can edit later. The concept is to bring into focus long buried or hidden information that you can comfortably examine now without any emotion or judgment. You are giving yourself the gift of reflective time to remember yourself as a little child, a teen-ager and an adult. Who were you then? Who are you today? And who do you want to be in the future? What is it you desire? Only you know the answers and only you will know the inner meaning of each occasion that you choose to include in your timeline.

After you have made this initial list, step away from the writing for a while, do something mundane or take a brisk walk to empty your mind. Then review your data again for any new input that may now simply pop into your mind. Because you are totally engaged, your memory and any deeply hidden emotions will begin to surface with new information for examination and possible additions. Continue to read your list again, editing and highlighting important dates and occasions that still have a strong emotional pull for you. Now, re-edit this first draft as concisely as possible, adding key adjectives for emphasis, stopping often to formulate just the right word to state exactly what you felt, then, and now. Force yourself to be brief and specific, reminding yourself that these are the absolute core events that have shaped your life. You are deeply opening your inner-self, to find out who you were, how you thought, how you acted and how you appeared to others.

As you continue treasure hunting, remind yourself that it is your good fortune to see with present clarity, that particular time and the emotional energy that hooked your memory. Try to be as dispassionate as possible; allowing yourself to simply accept what happened as a part of your life. You might want to ask the following questions: Why is this particular time or event in my life included? Is it a basic fact or something else entirely? Does it trigger a response that is positive or negative? Am I proud of this event and has it helped shape my life? Is it currently affecting me in some way? If its effect is still influencing my life negatively should I or can I give it up? Is it holding me back or pushing me forward?

As you continually encounter yourself this deeply, you may be surprised to find you are bringing up past issues that have an almost identical reflection in your present life! As you continue to examine your past you may find that you are still carrying worn out energies and beliefs that are no longer worth keeping. This is the introspective phase, where you can bring up all the important facts of your life to full frontal view, so be sure to include everything, even if it hurts! You are confronting yourself in print, where you can work with what you have prospected in a completely dispassionate way. Is there anything more to add or subtract? If not, the final draft of your personal life history timeline is now ready for entry in your journal.

Recognize Your Gifts

It is important to take an inventory of the special gifts you have received and developed throughout your life. Many of these gifts may not even be apparent to you. Perhaps you have beautiful eyes or a warm smile or you are patient and understanding. Generous qualities of character and an interesting personality are gifts that you may simply take for granted, unaware how important they are for your success every day of your life. These gifts or qualities that you possess may have either been originally nurtured by others, given to you as your natural birthright or you have created or discovered them through your life process. It is now time to take stock of what you own, your unique strengths and abilities.

Personal Assessment of Your Gifts and Talents

What are the spiritual, mental, emotional and physical gifts you received at birth or those that you have recognized as you grew older? Many may be the result of your environment, or your education. Consider your body's health and strength, your skills, talents, personality, mental capabilities, strength of character, emotional stability and special characteristics. In your journal make a list of at least twenty-five of your gifts. Yes, you will easily find this number and many more. As you make the list include what is generally true for you on a scale of one to ten. Ask yourself only positive, uplifting questions that may include the following:

What are my best attributes or characteristics?
What are my best abilities and skills?
What are my best mental and physical capabilities?
What are my best natural talents that I have developed?
What are my greatest assets that I have developed?
What are my assets and talents that mean the most to me?
Are there any new assets and talents that I am now recognizing and using?

At some point the inner voices of your ego will try to prevent you from being so complementary to yourself. Compassionately tell them you have important work to do and you will check in later. They will then usually disappear because you have acknowledged their presence.

I have a friend with wonderful organizational gifts who developed her own company some years ago from a very unique idea she conceived. She moved her business from a real office to a single cell phone! This allowed her to travel freely and move to the Historic town of Sonoma where she had always wanted to live. In her Sonoma home she is always surrounded by friends, she loves to cook and entertains easily and with great style. One day I told her how creative she was with her business, the great parties she gave and everything else she has done with her life. To my amazement she said she had always thought of herself as a businessperson and not at all creative. "No," she said, "I am not creative, my mind is too logical!" Well, as you can imagine, every time I heard one of her new business ideas or listened to another of her fun filled local stories I reminded her of her incredible creative gifts.

It took a full year, but finally she accepted the fact that artists are not the only people who can be creative. That was her belief! From then on it was so wonderful to see her inventive mind at work, taking painting classes where she excelled, expanding her career options outward in new directions. She is a role model for everyone around her with her many skills, abilities and her totally loving and giving personality.

Because it is hard to get enough distance from ourselves to see with any real clarity, it might be a good idea to ask an intuitive friend or family member to describe something creative about you personally or your way of working that they admire or what they see as a special character trait. You might ask them to point out an ability, or skill, or a positive attitude that they appreciate. You will probably be amazed that what they tell you does not resonate as a personal gift in your mind! In fact it may be hard for you to accept what they say, because your belief system may be set at a different level! As in the true story above, both our inherent gifts and beliefs can often affect our perceptions, so I do suggest you gather helpful information from others.

Recognize Your Beliefs

Throughout our individual lifetimes we develop a broad spectrum of beliefs that color most of our thoughts and resulting actions. Because our beliefs have helped forge the particular pattern of our lives, an understanding of their underlying power is necessary. Ask yourself the following questions and create some of your own: Are there certain beliefs or standards that I have personally selected to live by, and why? Do I live by a particular religious or ethical code? How strong is my adherence to the beliefs that I now hold so dearly? Do I have limiting beliefs? Do I have expansive beliefs? Are my beliefs helpful to others and myself? The following suggestions are offered to assist your discoveries. In each column choose the questions and beliefs that fit together the best or change them to fit closer to your beliefs.

Your Questions	Usually I Believe	Sometimes I Believe
About Yourself	I am interesting and talented	I am unimportant
About Other People	People are basically good	It is all their fault
About Your Nation	In the laws of my country	I have no individual voice
About Your Success	I am responsible for success	Nothing I do is successful
About Your Money	Money pours into my life	Not enough money
About Your Fears	I am not afraid	I am afraid to use my gifts
About Your Spirituality	There is a higher creative force	There is no higher power
About Your Health	I am strong and healthy	I don't have health/energy

Recognize Your Thought Patterns

We are what we think! What we think we become! Old adages, but true. Are your thoughts each day positive, negative or a mixture? Are you aware of any thoughts that may keep you trapped? Do you control your mind or does it control you? We rarely examine these daily thought patterns so this is the time to do so. Make a list of the thoughts that drift in and out of your consciousness today and then evaluate them. If there are too many worries or concerns, the spiritual guidance throughout this book will help rebalance your way of thinking so that your past, present and future can realign in harmony.

Mind States

To help make your list quickly name a thought that is passing through your mind and consider what mind state you are in, right now! Would you say it is: Happy mind, interested mind, accepting mind, skeptical mind, rejecting mind, or possibly neutral mind? Is your ego involved? Does your mind state confirm, jolt or deny any of your core beliefs? What did you discover about yourself? Was it easy to name both the thought and the mind state it came from?

If you begin to notice these fleeting thoughts and their reasons you will discover much that you did not know about yourself. Perhaps this morning you were sitting in a meeting, knowing you should be contributing, but you chose not to. Visualize looking back at yourself in the meeting and try to name what was driving your decision not to participate. Maybe it was lack of energy or you didn't feel well, but why? Perhaps your ego-self was just shy this morning, but why? Whatever you discover, name it, try it on for size, and then accept what you have learned without judgment. Below is just a sampling of the various mind states that we do experience every day.

Types of Mind States

A brief sample: Comparing mind, judging mind, expectant mind, eager mind, skeptical mind, resisting mind, disbelieving mind, neutral mind, accepting mind, hopeful mind, joyful mind, upset mind, trusting mind, happy mind, interested mind, approving mind, disapproving mind, envious mind, shy mind, scared mind, fearful mind, loving mind, peaceful mind, jubilant mind, wow mind, eureka mind, sad mind, restless mind, jealous mind, apprehensive mind, agitated mind, selfish mind, agonized mind, not good enough mind, I am better than mind, compassionate mind, I am wonderful mind, I am special mind.

What are the typical thoughts and mind states that you have discovered? Document the list in your journal for reference and evaluation. I have asked my guides for their advice?

> "What a person thinks often controls the life, for good or ill. Life is not always easy when the mind directs every action and concern, as it does not leave room for the greater view. There are other dimensions within each individual that can be accessed without thought. That is why clearing the mind with meditation and automatic writing is so important. They release the mind and its thoughts for awhile and allow other information, ideas and guidance to surface."

Your Ego-Self

The Universe Speaks: *"The ego is the inner part of you that gives direction and meaning to your life in a variety of ways. It is always conscious of the need for your self-fulfillment, supporting all your choices even though they may not all be beneficial. Because it supports everything that you do, if allowed total freedom, it can dominate your personality to the exclusion of friendship from others. It can lead to grandiosity and belief in self at the expense of all else.*

Working in partnership with the ego, asking it to marginalize its role, can lead to quiet and contentment—without always striving for success, which can never be totally accomplished anyway, because there is always the striving for more and more. Make peace with your ego, ask it to let you enjoy what you do with your life and ask it to support you in new ways to grow rather than push and criticize and pummel. The ego can be either a relentless aggressive power or a comfortable friend that supports your goals. Talk to and listen to your ego to know its agenda, discuss what you can achieve together and it will cooperate if you are serious. This may take several meditative sessions to accomplish. After all your ego has been in charge your entire life, until this point."

The strength of the ego-self, or the "I" that we present to the world, may lead us far along the path to personal success throughout our lives. In our behalf it continuously strives for the most perfect expression of our many unique gifts and abilities. Well intentioned, it is our great ally when life is going well and our demanding tormentor when life is not. When we hear an inner critic judging and scolding we know it is our ego in its many guises, continually trying to correct any major deviations from the original, possibly tattered script we dictated to our inner-selves long ago. As we become aware of the need for separation from those old scripts, the ambition of the ego to continue the old original way may produce internal disquiet and uncertainty.

Because our identity is so tied to our ego, believing this is who we truly are, it is easy to get stuck in both the desire for change and the fear of too much. This inner ambivalence may continue for years until we realize that allowing a dominating ego the freedom to lead the way is counter-productive to our new life goals. When we clearly see this divisiveness within ourselves, it is time to take a stand and ask the ego to redirect its talents in certain areas. I think you will find that the ego has several different voices.

Meditations with Your Ego

Discussion with Your Ego

Talking internally with your ego may seem a strange thing to do but it is amazing how well it works. Sit in meditation and project your thinking into your body, then internally say you would like to have a friendly discussion. Choose a theme and maybe say you would like the ego to be more supportive and not so aggressive or you would like your ego to be more assertive. Just listen placidly to the answers whatever they are. Your ego will probably say that it is only following your dictates. With this information you can decide what kind of support or resolution you want to make. How does your ego affect your life? Is it too strong or too submissive, creating problems of self-esteem? Is its control important for your success? Is your identity totally tied to your ego? Is there too much self-referencing in conversations with others? Is self-gratification a dominant motivation? Are there changes you would like to make?

Listen to Your Ego

Later, sitting in meditation, bring your attention and inner gaze to the warmth of your inner body, then to your heart, your lungs, your breath, your quiet hands, your resting feet, then back again to the whole of your body that is now very, very comfortable and totally at peace. Now ask your ego to come forward into your consciousness to be heard. You may hear several different voices so listen with great care to each one. You may need to say that this is a friendly forum with absolutely no agenda. Tell each voice that you are here to learn, not to dictate! If they are shy, be patient, you are building trust. Listen without interruption and when all are finished thank each one for sharing, and ask if you may listen again. Be sure to get their agreement, saying once again how much you appreciate their thoughts and ideas. You may notice the voice of your intuition, or your guides speaking occasionally, but please stay focused on your ego voices, as they have the starring role. If you can write while receiving you will retain much more of these inner dialogues.

Friendship with Your Ego

Begin the next meditative session in the same way, then ask your ego and its voices to come forward. This time discuss a topic of your choice or ask for their ideas. Letting your ego voices select a topic may bring up information that you would not even have considered as important. You will find they are much more agreeable to chat now that you have built their trust and honored their presence. I suggest you ask their names or give each one a representative title such as: the caretaker, the princess, the crusader, the nitpicker, the critic, the energizer, the tormentor, the controller, the perfectionist, etc.

Ask for Support from Your Ego

In the third session, now that you and your voices are comfortably communicating, ask them for their support or guidance or evaluation about your life path, or the comfort of inner harmony. Decide exactly what you need and ask for their continuing helpfulness in all you desire. If you feel resistance you may need to be very emphatic and state even more specifically that you do not need to work with outdated information or sad memories or impossible role models any longer—and to now release you. When your ego voices accept that you are truly serious you will feel a little click of comforting internal relaxation. Almost immediately a sense of peace, joy and new purposeful vitality will begin to surge throughout your body. You can now work together as friends, knowing your ego will support your decisions as long as they are in alignment with your chosen goals. Without your awareness your ego-self and its many voices may have long desired a more companionable role in your life and are now most thankful for this new partnership.

Life History Clearing Process

At the beginning of this chapter you developed a personal life history timeline. Now that you have worked deeply with your inner-self it is time to make some final determinations as a guide for your future. Begin by highlighting all the items that trigger very positive or extremely negative inner responses. Think of yourself simply as a reporter choosing only those that hit you immediately. After reviewing the highlighted areas ask yourself more questions: What effect has each event had on my life? What age was I? Where did this happen? What emotion do I feel about it now? Perhaps you have forgotten about something you loved to do and you now know you would like to bring it more fully into your life. Clearly state exactly what you desire and invite it to enter. Ask yourself whether any changes need to be made in your beliefs, your thought patterns, your ego-self or difficult lingering emotions.

A day or two later look again at your highlighted positive and negative issues, focusing on each one and allowing any further feelings or insights to well up. Hot button issues that once triggered strong responses may be gone, replaced by a whole new understanding of why they were so powerful. However, if there is still strong emotional pain attached to any of these issues, practice releasing it in the section below: (How to release emotional pain).

Now give yourself a refreshment holiday for part or all of the day. Let all your emotions flow out and away from your body—yell, scream, sing, dance, maybe create a moving meditation, throw a rock, do whatever is necessary. Talk to the birds and the sky, breathe in the freshness of the air, and smile at the sun or the snow or the rain, absorbing the peace that surrounds you. Let your inner-self match the refreshment you are experiencing as you connect with nature. Continue to release everything you may have stored or built up for possibly many, many years. Let it all out! Fling out all that energy and emotion, good or bad—whatever it is. When you are finished look up at the sky again and feel the softness of the air, the heat of the sun, or the wetness of the rain—surrounding yourself with peace and love.

When you are again ready, sit quietly and look dispassionately at each highlighted issue or event. Have a little inner discussion with whatever you decide to keep, develop further, or leave behind. Ask each issue several questions: Has it been useful in some way? Can you rely upon its support and growth in the future? Would it like to become more important in your life? Would it like to give up working so hard? If it is no longer useful or it is still affecting you negatively you need to say that you no longer need its presence in your life. Thank it for coming to your attention, and then just let it fade away.

Continue sitting quietly, letting any new answers percolate into your awareness. You may wish to congratulate a positive attribute that has newly surfaced to your attention, perhaps finding that it has been a secret foundation block of your life. If so, thank it for its sustenance and ask if it will be more available to your mind, body and spirit from now on. You may also want to ask its knowledge to increase or be more constructive in your life. Lastly give it the acceptance and praise it needs to continue directing its creative force into both your present and future life. Thank all of these important events and issues for coming to your attention, then just let everything go, drifting peacefully away as you inwardly visualize the silent riffles of a fresh mountain stream flowing slowly up and down throughout your body knowing you have cleansed your past and set your intentions on a new pathway.

Document Your Clearing Process

The last step is to document this clearing process into your journal—or you may prefer to jot down only trigger words and phrases as reminders for later completion. It is easy to forget the actual experience of inner work so I suggest you make your notes as soon as possible, then lay the whole thing aside for a week or two, offering it to your core-self and the Universe for further guidance.

How to Release Emotional Pain

Within yourself, bring forth the maximum amount of your emotional pain, experiencing it as deeply as possible and leaning into it strongly with all of your mind, heart and soul. Feel its intensity and torment for only a few minutes, then as much as possible withdraw your attention and focus on something entirely different for a while. When you are ready to begin again, lean strongly into the pain for a few more minutes as you did before, and then once again release. Continue to do this over a period of several days or weeks until you can no longer bear to go into the pain that deeply—you cannot put yourself through that torture any longer. Gradually you will find the deep emotional pain is gone and in its place is remembrance only, with maybe an occasional surface tingle of unpleasantness. You have dissipated the energy of the emotion within so that your mind can now relax its obsession with the problem and let it go. This process is not easy, but it brings resolution and a quiet end to possibly years of torment.

During a time of intense emotional crisis many years ago, I tried to find books to help guide my way back to sanity, but none offered relief. Finally I found that forcing myself in and out of the pain was the answer, and since then in a variety of situations that process has helped immensely.

Trust and Faith

God only responds to a peaceful heart! When we need a savior as a last resort we turn crying and pleading to God to save us. And have you noticed that there is usually no response? For the most part our prayers are primarily requests—for an increase in health, wealth, peace and personal happiness. When we hurt we pray!

The friendship we can have with God is similar to our earth relationships—close or distant, we would not think of asking for crisis assistance from a stranger. We would go to someone we trust. No, God does not lift us up and out of my suffering. We are usually too tied to our inner angst to let go and trust that all will be well.

For release bring heart-warmth energy into consciousness, step into the silence of meditation for a while, discuss your troubles if you need to with your guides and your inner Source, ask for support in resolving all issues, and finally thank your guides and God for listening and releasing the pain. Then simply let go and let God handle it!

Life Changes and New Goal Exercises

After completing the clearing process, if you would like to continue to change various aspects of your life or achieve new goals, the following exercises will be very useful and rewarding. Please consider all four aspects of your life: spiritual, mental, emotional and physical. Within the theatre of the mind, get ready to play with your imagination. Step outside your familiar belief and thought patterns long enough to visualize changes that can dramatically alter your life. Once created in imagination and accepted by mind, your aspirations can be acted upon by the intelligence of the Universe and brought into present reality.

The Process

Set your intent in writing. Change your thinking in line with your new goals. Begin purposeful action for their achievement. Relax and let the Universe do the rest. Before you begin, quiet your mind for a few minutes, then center yourself within, shut your eyes, make your loving heart connection, ask for guidance, breathe slowly and evenly, then gradually feel yourself settling into expansive openness and ask for changes you would like to make, knowing they will become a reality in some way.

Create Simple Achievable Goals

Choose a few simple goals that you want to achieve over the next three to six months. You will find if you select just a few for completion within a specific time limit there will be more success. Be sure to choose goals that are easily attainable to help you develop trust in the process. After they are chosen, the entire mechanism of the self begins to create a secret strategy for fulfillment. To assist in your final selection make three vertical columns. Title the first column Goals, the second column Advantages and the third column Concerns. Make your goal list as long as you wish, responding to each goal as either an advantage or a concern. Called the Benjamin Franklin Method, it is a wonderful procedure that allows you to present many more possibilities to yourself than you might have initially considered. When your goals are selected, actively participate in the achievement of each one in some small way. Remember, once you set your intention and activate it with action, the creative intelligence of the Universe will help produce it, possibly not to your exact specifications, but in a form that you will recognize.

These three columns are an example of this method:

Goals	Advantages	Concerns
Return to school	Education/better job	Time/money/age
Exercise regularly	Health/energy/weight	Time/money/disinterest
Take a vacation	Adventure/relax/play	Time/money/companions
Play a musical instrument	New directions/grow	Time/money/fear
New relationship	Companion/love/fun	Share/lose freedom
More time for self	Freedom/joy/less stress	Job/family/time
Buy a house	Security/pleasure/comfort	Price/not ready/location
Buy a car	Fun/comfort/prestige	Money/garage/need
Cultural events	Enjoy/learn/fun	Time/money
Complete projects	Satisfaction/pleasure	Time/fear
Volunteer	Pleasure/giving/knowledge	Energy/time/health

Re-Write Your Present Life

What is most important to you? What is your level of commitment for change if needed? What actual choices do you have? Daydream about any and all possibilities for a while, then close your eyes and visualize everything you desire in living color. Remember you can mentally create anything! Be extravagant, be wild, be zany, let your vision soar! Don't worry; your practical self will always be waiting! Creative, vivid visualization sets the stage for successful actualization! When you have come back to earth, document your experience in your journal, then sit back and let your practical self go to work creating. Finally, set your intent for these changes in your life and thank your inner-self! Trust that the Universe will support all you desire, then relax, knowing it will be accomplished, possibly in new ways that you can not now foresee or even anticipate.

Produce Your future

Stretch your wings. Be outrageous! How far can you pull your imagination? Forget conformity, money, abilities or reality for a while. Play with ideas, distant lands—you can go anywhere with your wonderful imagination. Play and visualize whatever you desire. There are no rules to hold you down. If you later decide to be practical, then plan what it is you want that is attainable, set your intent to create whatever you have chosen, then relax knowing you are on your way. It is not necessary to keep your mind focused on the successful achievement of your plan. Once you set your intention in writing and expect success, the Universe will totally support this second act of your life and flow consistently toward your intention.

The Universe Speaks

Love is the Heart of the Universe

"Expansion of Gifts
Creation is a living force, an endless cycle that you can and do participate in. Expansion of your inherent gifts to create is greatly magnified as you open fully to awareness of your divine connections. Carefully placing loving awareness of our Presence into each of your hearts will bring, in time, a magical transformation of your life experience. We love you with all our hearts forever. Life mirrors your individual choices.

Chosen Goals

> *To create chosen goals, sit quietly each day magnifying the power within, glowing it upward to us through your mind and heart. Reflect on your higher purpose of love and giving. Proceed steadily toward all of them, filling everything with love and light and they will come.*

Inner Attunement

> *Each individual yearns for knowledge and participation in certain fields of interest. There is no pre-recorded plan. As a life turns in its own orbit, changes can and do occur based on environment, health and world events. Remember, your personal life is always directed spiritually. Inner voices call you to certain investigations but the actual directions you take are your very own. As you decide to come consistently for inner attunement your specialized aspirations will begin to unfold congruently with your basic core-seed patterning."*

Document in Your Journal

Documenting the exploration of your life experiences in writing is vital to impress your conclusions firmly in memory. This is the chapter where documenting is incredibly important and I suggest you date the pages and maybe make little simple drawings in color to remind you of particular days and events. I hope this treasure hunt, to find out more about yourself and to help release old unnecessary memories and events, has been greatly rewarding and nurturing—with new goals now planned from the center of your unique self.

CHAPTER ELEVEN

RELEASE YOUR INNER CREATIVITY

Fling Wide Your Soul

Frieda and Valto speak: *"Creativity is an ever-flowing river that runs through all creation. It begins with the Creator moving forward into all that it creates. Each individual has the potential for development of gifts that were given before birth, and life on earth is greatly enhanced and beautified through the extension of these gifts outward into the population. Tell your readers; if they listen internally for guidance, they will open to their inner gifts in new and unexpected ways. If each creative endeavor is entered into from this center-ness of love, the result will be pure and true."*

This eleventh key helps expand your unique creative gifts to give your marvelous spirit its full expression. The many projects, which have evolved from several of these chapters, are intended to increase your appetite for joyful and introspective time to develop new skills and move new interests forward, for yourself and others.

As you continue to deepen your connection to the consciousness of the Universe it is now time to explore what you have learned in each chapter, in new creative ways. To help with this process I have made some choices for you in a series of special projects. Subtly you are being lead to expand beyond what you have learned. I asked the Universe for more information about creativity and imagination:

"You are constantly using your imagination to bring you closer to the realization of your dreams that awaken internally, seemingly from nowhere. Let your imagination lead you to explore new issues and new wonderments—you will miss them with only your mind as the leader. Let your imagination fling wide your soul to new exploits that will grow bolder and better with time. Explore the fantasy within, and lead yourself forward to catch your dreams. We accompany you on the way and are indeed more present when in the company of creative ideas with wings. Creativity is always accompanied by imagination. Begin with your meditation, tap into your loving Inner Presence, then fly away—we will be with you. This is always true, no matter who you are or what you have done—once you have tapped into our electrical frequencies, we are there guiding. We honor your desire to be with us and to expand beyond the boundaries that you may have unintentionally set for yourself."

How creative are we in our day-to-day thinking? Often we move forward so quickly with our plans that we forget to include creative options? We are so used to using a mind only approach that we forget to excavate the wealth of our intuitive, imaginative and unconscious selves. Learning to engage and channel these creative forces is the key to exposing what we often deeply hide from ourselves. As you consider the possibilities for each of the following group of projects, begin with spiritual support by quietly going within to center yourself, connect with your heart-warmth, ask for inner guidance and then wait until images or words or ideas move into the window of your imagination. Choose to be a patron for the support of your creativity by providing ample space, time, equipment and perhaps, special music.

A poem about creativity by Frieda and Valto.

"CREATIVITY

Creativity is the stuff of dreams
As glimpses of ideas
Glisten in the mind.
Visions surface with images,
Sound and movement.
Waiting expression
They tiptoe forward through
Secret passages of the soul.

Creativity exists in each
And everyone waiting for
The touch of recognition,
Often shut away for years in
Stuffy attics of the mind.
Then out it comes to
Illuminate each life with
Beautiful, individual expression."

Create from Inner Presence

Send Healing Energy

Before sleep, feel the sweetness of love flowing throughout your body as you usually do. Drift along for a while within its richness, simply enjoying the inner glow of love's light throughout your body. Then project what you are feeling out into space as a dense white glowing ball of healing to a person in need of its energy and light. Pull it totally over her/him and know that while inside, the healing is underway and will continue throughout the night.

Imagination and Emotions Exercise

A creative way to explore opening to your Inner Presence is to experiment with a variety of emotions. First imagine feeling very sad, perhaps bringing tears to your eyes. Now imagine feeling very happy, maybe even laughing. Now imagine being deeply, emotionally in love with someone. Then imagine being deeply in love with both yourself and your spiritual Source. Place your hand on your heart and ask this sweetest of emotions to be ever present there and available whenever needed.

Create a Heart-Warmth Energy Symbol

Create a symbol of your experience of the warmth within your heart and place it somewhere in your home where you can benefit from its presence. It can be anything that has meaning for you, something you already own or decide to create. It could be a photograph, a collage of special mementoes, poems or sayings, a painting maybe including a heart and a flame. When completed, talk to your newly created symbol to give it your special benediction and ask it to lend its loving energy to your life.

Create a Spiritual Vacation

"Just Let Go for Seven Days!
Make a calendar and mark each day with one act of commitment to elevating your divinity another notch. Let us be with you daily, with no agenda. Loving energy passing back and forth—illuminating your heart with light and warmth and thanksgiving.

Live with us each of these days in an uplifted way as much as you can. Resonate with the trees, with nature, in your garden, in your house—love your life and your surroundings.

Give up all fear of the future; give up all resentment and jealousy. Talk to your ego and ask for its cooperation. Tend only to your inner spirit, your spiritual growth, your physical self, and release everything else."

Create a Sitting Meditation

Dedicate the meditation to physical parts of your body or to an emotion. Ask each one what is needed and listen carefully as each one responds. Really listen, tuning in deeply to your physical body and your emotions—for as long as it takes—with no judgment whatsoever. Document the Presence in the aftermath of the glow of your meditation. If your experience is difficult to write just capture single words on paper that have meaning for you, then finish later. Draw any images of your body or emotions you saw or felt that are important to remember. Perhaps each part of yourself would like to say something? What was of most importance about this special meditation? Perhaps you might want to add color to your drawings.

Create a Moving Meditation

Go for a walk or a dance in a quiet natural setting. Be totally in the moment with the woodland and with the trees and the tiny wildflowers that may surround you. Touch the trees, feeling their internal energy, walk the path feeling your feet pressing into the resilient earth as you move. You may want to name certain trees, feeling the different textures of their bark and smelling the fragrance of each one. You may choose to dedicate this area as a sacred space, marking it with a name of its own in your journal. Return home with sacred woodland energy in your bones.

Create a Moss Garden for Meditation

Perhaps you have found some bright green moss and a seedling pine or two for a dish garden. Do you have a low dish or platter and some dirt to construct with? Do you have a mirror for a lake and something for a bridge or pebbles for a path? Are there any tiny Japanese bridges, temples or little plastic animals in your stored treasures? In a state of meditation, working with these materials, feel their different energies responding to your hands. When you are finished you may want to use it as a focus for meditation. These lovely moss gardens can last a long time if watered regularly.

Create a Personal Shrine for Meditation

In a state of meditation make an indoor or outdoor shrine with materials from your home or walking in nature meditations. What ideas do you have that would fit the personality of your home? Do you have a table or a box or a drawer that you can transform with paint and decorate in some way? See what you can find that is really interesting to you. As you work on your shrine ask it where it would like to be placed and what would it like to be used for? What would it like to display or honor? What does the word shrine mean to you?

For ideas you might look at the very colorful folk art shrines and the tin nichos from Mexico. Or the Japanese small red outdoor shrines that often hold fruit or figures of the Buddha. They are hung at eye level on the exterior of buildings throughout Kyoto. The word shrine in *Webster's Dictionary* is defined as a case, box or niche where sacred relics are deposited or a place in which devotion is paid to a saint or deity.

Dedicate Your Moss Garden and Shrine

When you have finished creating your moss garden and shrine you can dedicate each one with something special like music, fragrance, candlelight, a silent or spoken message, a dance, or a celebration feast. Also you can honor each one with a few more moments of your personal attention, thanking each one for this new energy that is enriching your personal environment.

Create by Intuitively Listening Within

Listen Within for Creative Ideas

Think about any kind of creative or unusual ideas you have been considering but have been afraid to undertake. Sit quietly for a few minutes, emptying your mind and breathing in your loving Inner Presence—in and out, in and out. Now silently draw your ideas into your inner-self, explaining the pros and cons and expect to receive a response. Within a short time whispered words will begin flowing through your consciousness; however, they may at first be garbled or incorrect. Just wait patiently and expectantly, possibly restating your ideas in a different way. Soon new words will start drifting through your mind containing creative thoughts about each idea.

Listen Within while Traveling

Plan a trip or choose a few free hours or a day to drive somewhere without pre-planning. Empty your mind, breathe deeply and bring in your shimmering Inner Presence. Tell your inner voices you are open to their suggestions about where to go, what to do along the way and that you will follow their suggestions faithfully. After they have offered their ideas and you have begun your trip, continually stay in touch with your inner voices and ask for more directions. You may be very surprised at the route you will take and the experiences you will have.

Listen Within to Expand Your Writing Skills

Word clusters stretch your imagination, release your creative juices, and jump start expressive writing. Have fun with this process by asking your inner voices to supply all the words in the cluster and then help you organize them into an action scene, short story or poem, as suggested below. Ask them to whisper as many words as they can and form them into a word cluster with one subject word in the center. Off the wall thinking like this is often used to develop stories, plays, poems, visual imagery, etc.

Example of a single word cluster:

clinging, partners, energy, stop, go, fun, ancient, life, close, costumes,
hot, moment, beats, modern, alone, wild, crazy, sexy,
twirling, personal, steps, cha-cha, music,
syncopated, rhythm, fresh,
happy, fox trot, happy

DANCING
free, sticky, ugh, moving,
bending, whole body, fresh, arms, legs,
hours, leaves, rain, rumba, tango, nothing, boys,
girls, men, women, orchestras, instruments, wild, silly, violins

Creative cluster writing Ideas:

1. Produce several one-line descriptions of action scenes from the cluster.
2. Develop a one-paragraph short story. Example: I go wild with the sexy hot cha-cha rhythms as I freely move within clinging partners, dancing wildly in the sticky rain.
3. Write a 3 line non-rhyming poem.

Create with Stream of Consciousness Writing

Creative Stream of Consciousness Writing with Music

Listening to music is a natural way to enter into an altered state in preparation for stream of consciousness writing. Choose music that is inspirational, soothing, meditational or joyous and let your imagination float wherever it pleases for a while. Mentally join the birds and clouds in the sky and imagine flying along. When you are ready, begin with an internal question to the Universe, then let what you are receiving drift along with the rhythm of the music. Listening to music is always a wonderful way to open the creative channel to more inspiration. You can record what you are internally hearing by hand or with a computer. You could also experiment speaking into a recorder.

Creative Public Speaking

You may be asked to share your stream of consciousness writing experiences with a small or large group. Begin by speaking into a tape recorder, to hear if you speak with clarity and animation. Is your personality coming through? When planning the talk, first make notes of the overall goal, then finalize the notes as simply as possible. Just before speaking, attune yourself to your Inner Presence, then let everything go—trusting that the Universe will assist you in expressing what is needed for the audience to hear. Speak extemporaneously if you can because it makes a far greater impact.

Create Poetry

Ask for poems about a particular subject and let go, waiting to see what the Universe will give you. You might also study the way poems are constructed and ask for narrative or rhyming descriptions. You can of course keep your request totally open as I did. It would be very interesting to write poems within the stream of consciousness state on a walk or hike where you will not be disturbed. Walking along the bluffs above the ocean, then sitting down with a writing tablet, letting your mind flatten out to nothingness and waiting—should be enough for the whispers to begin. You might also think about asking the Universe for bits of information in the Japanese poetic form of Haiku. The first and last lines each have 5 syllables and the middle line has 7 syllables. The topics are usually about the different seasons or personal impressions. I have never asked for Haiku but it is another way to expand and explore your stream of consciousness writing.

Create with Life Experiences

Create a Personal Myth

Write about a self you may have discovered in Chapter Ten, Transform Your Life Experiences. Can you write a myth or fairy tale about the basic meaning of your life as you now see it? Can you fit your story into one of the Universal hero or heroine stories that are a part of our collective consciousness? Eric Berne wrote: "There are only a limited number of possible ways to live your life and they have all been encapsulated in myth and fairytale. There are many to choose from: Sleeping Beauty, Snow White, Cinderella, Goldilocks, The Frog Prince, Jason and the Golden Fleece, Parsifal, Beowulf, Sir Gawain and Lady Ragnell and all the God and Goddess stories."

As you reviewed your life perhaps you found that like Sleeping Beauty, you are just now awakening from a deep sleep of some kind, or that you are waiting to be rescued with a better job, or the right opportunity, or the right companion. Or you may discover that yours is a hero story, with parallels to the long complicated journey of Parsifal who chose to suffer through a series of perilous trials before becoming worthy enough to find "The Holy Grail."

Create your mythic story. What is your mythic name? What was the event or crisis that started you on your transformational journey? Who were your companions and did you meet anyone new? Do you have a dark side and a light side or a male and female self? What was the place like where you began? Where did you go? Who and what did you encounter? And then what happened?

Create Your Personal Symbol

Choose a personal symbol that stands for your idea of yourself. Perhaps this will be easy after creating your mythic story. If not, you might ask yourself what image would represent your nature and your ideals in the most meaningful way. Possible choices might be animals, birds, sun, moon, Tarot card images, birth year Chinese animal symbols, flowers, an image in a painting, etc. Why not draw or paint your symbol, frame it in some way and place it in your personal environment as a reminder to remain true to your inner spirit? If you like to work three-dimensionally, your symbol can be molded or shaped in a variety of self-hardening clay and paper sculptural materials from art and craft stores. There are lots of possibilities, depending upon your interests and resources.

Create a Collage Cover for Your Journal

A collage is a group of carefully or casually arranged images glued onto a surface to make a work of art. If you are using a standard size hard cover notebook for your journal with possibly a clear plastic sleeve for the insertion of imagery, create a collage that might include your personal symbol. Assemble it with non-wetting glue, then paste it directly on the hard cover or slip it into the plastic sleeve. You can also color copy the collage and laminate it for permanence. With creative computer software you can easily create a cover from your own gallery of images. If you are a photographer, a single favorite image could be placed into the clear plastic pocket.

Illustrate Your Journal Pages

Drawing little visual pictures in your journal beside your entries helps to remember that particular time and place in an instant of recognition. There is no need to be elaborate with your drawings, just a little stick figure here, a little wobbly table there, just enough to recognize the connection. Buying a few colored pencils helps identify a circle as a sun or squiggly lines as water, etc. Perhaps your artist-self would like to make your pages sing with color.

The Universe Speaks

Love is the Heart of the Universe

"*Creative Thought*

Creativity begins with an idea and an ability you know you have. You are never alone in your undertakings because the energies and intelligence of the Universe are ever in attendance, blending with your desires and fanning the flames of your enthusiasm to complete what you have chosen to achieve. Creativity often remains internalized without a visible presence in the world. All thought is a form of creation; this is why your thought is so potent. The more energy you give to the thought, the more Universal energy coalesces around it for completion.

Creative Development

To develop the idea, motion must occur in the form of energies and magnetic vibrations that begin to coalesce around it. The person, feeling the energy, puts forth effort in the form of investigation of the subject and the development of its potential. As this creative person continues faithfully and diligently to develop the idea,

Universal energy and intelligence combine to bring it into fruition.

Create Freely

Use all you have been given with great delight. You are created to be happy and to receive the bounty of earth's offerings, plus the offerings of your own body and mind. Use them freely! What magical things you can create. How extraordinary your ability to create through your mental and intuitive self.

God Speaks

Life was given to you to grow your abilities as far as possible. You are meant to be happy, to enjoy life, to experience with pleasure the beauties of your natural world. All that you can make and imagine I want you to express outward with the sheer pleasure of being alive.

How to Achieve

Whatever the project, begin with love. Meet all possibilities, all projected plans from your still-point center of love—the flame of joy and ecstasy in your heart. Create all that you desire from this place and you will achieve beyond all your expectations.

Working with Clay

When you work with clay, imagine it as alive and growing under your hands. Give it your spirit of love and attention."

Frieda and Valto have written a poem about clay.

"CLAY

Clay is soft, enduring, pliable, ready
For adventures with the hands and
Feet and anything else that could
Make new magic's.

Your clay expressions are your own,
Your moods, your resistances, your
Interplay with the elements
Of earth and water.

Clay speaks a language of its own
Soft and pliable though it is.
It speaks through your hands upward
Into forms of beauty and strength,
Evoking the radiance of your soul's
Path into the unknown.

Just play, bringing your best fun self
To the clay, shaping, twisting, spiraling,
New adventures for the eye to see.
The burnished gold of sun winged goblets,
The shining altar of higher attunement.

Soon you will find in your blood
A warmth of nonresistance,
Expressing outward into sureness of
Touch as new ideas emerge,
Tantalizing your senses."

Document in Your Journal

Each one of these creative projects can be explored in a variety of different ways and I know you will think of new ones as you continue to choose those that are the most meaningful for you. As usual, document each project; write your comments about your process, thoughts, and any other information that might be helpful in the future. By this time you will have found out much more about your own creativity through the projects offered here and the creative process of writing in your journal. Perhaps it is time to think about writing your own book about your spiritually creative adventures!

EPILOGUE

When I decided in 2001 to write a book about my beautiful and inspirational spiritual adventures with the Universe I had no idea how meaningful the actual writing would be for me personally, because my only goals had been to share the powerful messages and poems that I was given, and to share the incredible secret of divine Inner Presence. So my continuing spiritual growth has been a great blessing and I am deeply thankful. Throughout the writing my greatest treasures have been my spiritual guides and invisible friends, Frieda and Valto. My reverence and love for them is really indescribable. Now, with publication, this totally private life we have had together will end, and perhaps that is why completion of this book is not at all easy. Recently, however, the Universe has been subtly prodding me to get on with the publishing. I am being told that it is not enough to make what I have received over these years my own private kingdom forever.

My heart surges forth with great gratitude to have been entrusted as the keeper of this Universal wisdom for so long, and to now be the messenger to help spread its great truths. In a way, as I look back at this remarkable adventure with the Universe, it feels like a series of garden stepping stones laid one after the other, often haphazardly, but continually stretching out into the sweetness and mystery of the unknown. Very much like a garden of vast fertile energy, creativity, intelligence and love that has brought its own sweet rewards as each chapter has continued to unfold. My hope is that *The Secret of Inner Presence* will find fertile soil in the hearts of all who desire a greater, more illumined life.

My journals are the foundation of this book. Without them none of the dialogues or meditations would have been documented, and this book could never have been written. The real beauty of doing that writing forced me to take the time to save what I was receiving in the moment, and to describe thoughts and insights that often just flickered through for a sparkling instant before dissolving in the mist of memory.

Frieda and Valto would you be willing to write a poem for the ending of our book?

"Yes we will be happy to,

UNITY

Come unto us, come unto us,
Each and every one.
We are here waiting for your call.
Stretch beyond yourselves
Into the unknown from which you came
For access to our love and knowledge.

Love is indeed the heart of the Universe.
Each of you is a part of that love,
But only a part of the whole, the unity,
The puzzle of the pieces all fitting together,
Then our work is done.

We love you with all our hearts
Beckoning you home again
When you are ready.

_____Goodbye only for now,
Frieda and Valto"

"You are connected to the natural world and
the cosmos in which you live.
___The Universe Speaks"

APPENDIX

MY JOURNALS

The journals of my joyous illuminating adventures with the Universe were begun to document all the stream of consciousness messages and poems that I was receiving, including my inspiring inner growth through meditation, and my life experiences as I began to spiritually transform both internally and externally. Some of those early entries and current ones as well are offered here to demonstrate how important it is to accurately describe what is most important in the moment. It is also fascinating to read the descriptions and insights months and years later. My journals are in a very real sense my silent partners that have long held the necessary information I needed to write this book.

Journal Entries

Contentment

This afternoon, I feel more whole than I ever remember feeling in my entire life. I am certain that the key is consistently practicing inner connection through meditation and the heart-warmth connection. I am amazed how far I have come into peace and serenity in such a short time. Of course no one sees the difference but I feel so very content knowing absolutely all is well in my life within God's guidance. What will come of these daily engagements that are evolving naturally without my interference?

Writing

What am I doing, sitting here writing about God and my life and my inner truths, right in the midst of Christmas? Presents to buy, house to decorate, Christmas cards to write, real estate clients to call—but I sit and write anyway. Yesterday I wrote for seven hours almost non-stop! I just sat down with no warning Sunday at high noon jotting an outline for "the book" in a new notebook. When I began there was no clear idea those thoughts would continue to grow into an ordered manuscript with chapters and headings. I just simply began, emptying ideas onto paper.

This continual writing is even more amazing to me because my interests and actions for months have been totally focused on creating collages and experimenting with encaustic wax processes in my newly reorganized garage/garden studio. Going to Seattle for Thanksgiving to be with my daughter and grandchildren must have broken that creative cycle because now one week to the day since my return the words are flowing fast and free, as if there is some pent-up demand for them to be set loose at last. Oh, to be two people and do it all beautifully.

I have always been fascinated with an artist's notes and working processes that lead up to a finished painting or musical composition or book. Usually the audience or reader never gets to share that creative journey and is presented only with the final polished vision. So why not, I thought, include all the actual thinking, meditating and journal writing in my book, warts and all! In this way I will be able to communicate my own experiences as they happen and each reader may accompany me on the day-by-day journey. We can share together, each growing side by side.

Evening

I love my house so much! Paper Shoji Temple lanterns glowing, fire in fireplace so friendly with leaping flames warming, Shami asleep in her basket, my paintings and ceramics all about—a visual declaration that because they exist my artist-self exists, tall plants green and healthy, me so in thrall of this invisible spiritual quest in the beauty of the night.

Earth-Time

This morning, driving to yoga I decided that daily journal writing and recording my heart-warmth meditations for at least a month will be my intensive creative work this winter season. Totally engaging myself in this day-to-day commitment could enrich many peoples' lives if I were to include it all in the book I have been thinking about writing for so long. At a kind of subconscious level it is becoming quite obvious that I feel pretty dedicated to writing it. Thinking back to meeting Frieda and Valto, I am once again aware that length of time is of no consequence to spirit. I fret about time wasted but to the Universe there is no concern for the length of earth-time involved.

My Inner and Outer Life

French doors all open, blue jays and crows cawing, Canadian geese flying overhead in formation, Shami asleep as usual these days, real estate calls completed—now, the whole day to myself, soaking in the soothing tranquility of this golden fall! The whole month has been a gift of perfect Indian summer! A very dry season and concerning for our fire fighters, but for people like me, who dread closed doors and cooling temperatures, these quiet sun filled autumn days are perfection, like a freshly picked Macintosh apple held to the cheek, warm from the sun.

Each day when I awaken, it is just the normal me, feeling great or neutral or full of whatever is scheduled for the day. Then, almost as if I had forgotten, I look out at the trees and instantly I am transported to the "land of sweetest love." Lying there for ten or fifteen minutes within that glowing place of perfect peace is absolute perfection.

Then I come back, take Shami out for her walk and begin my day, but in any instant, at any time if I choose, I can be transported inward again to perfect peace and love without missing even a tiny beat of my practical life. I have recognized this transference between inner and outer since my gift of awakening, realizing that I live in two worlds that are intertwined—the one visible, the other real only to my inner-self. The invisible world is becoming totally blissful as more and more of my divine-self emerges. The visible world inhabited by my human physical-self is not always that easy to live with, but it also is becoming more peaceful as my two selves blend or perhaps I should say, balance.

I remain very much my physical self in group interaction, or when totally focused on a project or book or movie, but when I choose to tune inward I can instantly merge with spirit. It is such a blessing in my life! It would be so wonderful if everyone could have this same experience, and maybe many people will through my book? What a different world it would be! It is my hope that each reader will feel drawn into this state through what I have written. The writing of this book has been and is continuing to be a great teacher for me—with each of the chapters I grow. At first it was difficult writing from my own core knowledge. Stream of consciousness writing is so much easier leaning on the Universe to explain the unknowable or asking Frieda and Valto to offer their insights!

Veils

Lying in bed in the beauty and warmth of my shimmering Inner Presence wrapped in this consuming joyous light that pervades my entire being! The more I am continuously in this enveloping tender space the more I want to stay for longer and longer periods of time.

Searching

I am continually being drawn to go beyond the veils of my personal existence and on into knowledge of the mystery of mysteries. I read inspirational books, listen to enlightened speakers, questionable psychics and people who are channeling higher vibrations. I have also tried traditional meditation in a group setting occasionally. One of those adventures was in Kyoto, Japan, sitting with my son and several monks on hard wooden platforms outside an ancient temple. We sat seemingly for hours, both of us unable to keep our thoughts quiet and our eyes shut. I have beautiful memories of that time, secretly watching through half closed eyes the peaceful silent monks and the beauty of the red maple trees glowing all around us.

Meditation, Healing

Working with healing, hands warmed from breathing energy into them, relaxed easily, released all external pressures, thanked the Universe for the beauty and serenity of our precious time together, softly breathed love in and out, in and out, over and over. Gradually I felt so peaceful and so content just to be quiet with myself. Stayed with this feeling for a while until an all-enveloping white glow surrounded my head and appeared behind my eyes. This was the first time the inner light had been so luminous, it was absolutely incredible! I then tried to see images but couldn't, tried also to warm my hands with the light and they became warmer. Finally I did see layers of white gauzy veils in front of an ornate old-fashioned altar with a smooth ivory Madonna face in the distance. Then the veils were all swished away to become a clear dark void with an altar and the remote smooth faced Madonna shining softly in the misty distance. I sat, just sat lingering, happy and content. No need to do anything.

God

Prayer was the only way I was taught as a child to reach God. Dutifully I prayed each night asking for things, saying little prayers. In all those young years I never listened to God and although I felt very close it never occurred to me to give God equal time to possibly speak to me! Somehow, many years later in adulthood I did learn to listen and that has made all the difference!

Choice to Receive

I have learned many new things since receiving my gift of self-love. Illuminating information may be given to us and it may appear that we have been chosen to receive it. However, to expand the horizons of this new awareness we must use what we have been given, integrating it into our daily lives or it withers away from lack of use. God, divine energy, the higher self, does not do the work for us! We are not suddenly divine beings, blessed with perfect knowledge and perfect lives! We make the choice to interconnect the natural visible world with the spiritual invisible world or not. We can work in partnership with divine intelligence, but our higher power never takes over and lives our lives for us. Or even smoothes the path ahead consistently.

Deities and Evil

Eyes open, sun shining, golden radiance outside surrounding the oak trees and inside my inner-self. I asked about evil, the concept of inherently evil people and felt the answer:

> "There are both good and evil in the invisible Universe. There is no actual heaven or hell. Evil is a force; it is also a choice we can make at any time in our lives. Evil exists and we must disperse its energy, not let it enter our bodies or give it any opportunity. We must remain God centered always believing in our spiritual perfection."

Listening Within

Sweeping tons of oak leaves off both my front and back patios. Beautiful warm fall day once again. Just to be outside raking leaves is the perfect activity for this quiet contemplative day. While sweeping I decided I might listen for Frieda and Valto and ask if I could seek their advice on common little every day things like making decisions, warning me of danger, guiding my choices. It seemed very presumptuous but they could always say no.

"They whispered, *this is why we are here. Of course we will advise and guide you.*"

Meditation, Transformation

Brought love forth and relaxed in its warmth, thought about self-love. If we love ourselves fully and completely, knowing we are love, we can expand it into everything, which then becomes a circle, a continuous loop. Please dear God help me to be faithful to my inner-self. I am so happy and so fulfilled within your embrace of love. Here I am in the autumn of my life and just now finally getting serious about transformation! Frieda and Valto just whispered,

> *"Go now and work with your paintings. It is a good thing that you bring your other creative selves back to life. What you are experiencing on an inner level is meant to make you whole. Do not think of us as a daily commitment, but daily joyful attunement to the Universe."*

Meditation Difficulty

The familiar flow of love began but only peripherally. I felt compressed, trying too hard, wanting to do my meditation and then get it over with, off to finish some of the paintings before my son Brad arrived.

> *"This is a good lesson learning to be with other people and still be able to release to our Universal love. Just stay with us five more minutes, commit to that! See a stream running right through you, bubbling, little fishes, orbs of light, water tumbling, singing over stones as it rushes through, tumbling in delight. It is a happy clear stream, cleansing, releasing your hold on events of the day. Just let it wash through and feel our golden light of love surrounding you and spreading outward."*

Thank-you God and Frieda and Valto. I love you!

Meditation, Angel

I relaxed on the couch, shut my eyes, felt the richness of this union within merged with spirit. I asked to see the altar of higher attunement. A structure appeared on my left with no details, a pathway in the distance. A white searing light continued to pulsate. At its most intense I mentally beamed it to Shami for continued healing and asked an angel to lay hands upon her. The angel bent over her in her bed, laid her hands around her for a short time and then opened her body and smoothed all her internal organs through the bloody tissue. She finally closed her stomach with no scar, no blood and said the poisons were removed and she would now heal. She moved back to her place behind me. I thanked the angel for the healing of everyone I had been in contact with during the meditation. I also gave thanks for this free day to spend with spirit, taking me higher and higher. It was really, really hard to come back, so I stayed in this blissful state for a while longer just resting in the peace of it.

Meditation, Inner Love

Closing my eyes, I asked to feel love intensely. Inwardly I said and deeply felt my magic words, "I love you God, I love myself," immediately warm melting love sped in gently, enveloping me in its folds. Pink light began pulsing behind my eyes. I decided to project loving a lover, feeling throughout my body the joy we would have together, and the waves of love increased a hundred fold. I then brought all this emotion back into myself, filling my body completely with the sweetest happiness imaginable. The pink light grew brighter, dancing happily; rays of love coming in stronger and stronger holding me tight. I thought how incredible it would be to live this way constantly, walking alone on the beach, driving with good friends, going to bed alone but not alone. So I visualized these normal events—seeing myself walking on a high bluff overlooking the ocean listening to the rhythmic crashing of the waves, driving with friends, then a message came through the pink throbbing light,

"Love ebbs and flows, ebbs and flows. The beach water at the ocean rushes out tinkling the sand and little stones, then crashes back in, sweeping you up in its power."

Love's Ebb and Flow

Sitting in the sun remembering the intensity of my emotions during that meditation I thought, there is no way I can carry that intensity of feeling in every action of my day. Today, though, I will see if I can, and maybe even drive to the beach. Perhaps the ocean message stands for the power of love that naturally ebbs and flows, or for an emotional love that can consume dangerously.

The Ocean's Message

Do you have thoughts on love, the crashing ocean and tinkling sand and stones?

"Yes we are with you. Just let your pen walk across the page spinning out our thoughts one by one. We were with you in this morning meditation spilling out our love in bucket loads, drowning you in searing beauty. The singing sand and stones, the crashing water are all pictures to hold in your mind for your future use to remember love's message of majesty and power, then release, if necessary. No one can hold the searing intensity of love for too long a time. The flames would burn you up, thus the cooling water. Do you see, sea?

Your interpretation as a human is correct because you are inside that life and know its form. Our perspective is bigger, broader, which is what you are requesting; a bigger, enhanced view of the Universe. You are tired of your cramped little steps you think, you want more and more and so you shall have. Your steps are not cramped, not little, but steps only to the broader view. You must do the inner work of preparation. We have missed these sessions. Go now with your lovely day."

Meditation, Stay Centered

Difficult to receive the unconditional love usually flowing through my heart. Love's flame was still on low no matter how I tried to strengthen its energy! I asked my guides for advice, apologizing for a week of laziness. Sitting waiting I felt the following,

> *"Stay centered each moment of your day in every activity within the warmth of your heart. You began growing it, flowering it into your life, then its intensity merged with the joy of your inner journey and you accepted this as growth. You let go of the center of your being without realizing it! It has been weeks since you have felt the intensity of your total loving heart.*
>
> *Begin each day centered in love's light, keeping it alight and glowing outward and inward in each and every interaction. Think not of results you desire, only your oneness with all of creation and the joy of connection. The results will happen without effort or ceremony along the way. The choice is always yours, which do you choose, living only your visible easily recognizable earth-self or expansion through discourse with the invisible world that contains all knowledge, all love? Can you really go back now, having traveled this far? Shall you give us all up, easily going back to being separate once again? We think not, for you will feel our tug, our pull toward home where you belong."*

Walking Meditation

Mexico: Dear Frieda and Valto and all the Universal masters, what can I do to connect with you without having to close my eyes to the world or go into meditation?

> *"With open eyes, walk along the beach this morning, forgetting your physical self and its needs and blend yourself into the fish and birds and rocks and sea. Magnetize your vision into everything and experience it*

all as love. Go forth now and experience what you feel, knowing we are with you in this, guiding your search. Part of your growth is to stay within your goal of greater intimacy and connection. This is your practice which, if faithfully followed, will heighten your awareness of All That Is and become yours for a lifetime."

So I walked slowly and deliberately down to the beach, looking deeply at the beauty of everything I saw. My footsteps in the sand felt very light and uplifted, the pelicans' with their sparkling throats filled with fish soared and dove all around me, every grain of sand, every person, every coconut palm tree appeared radiant. It seemed impossible to ever return to walking briskly again without looking at each and every bird and rock and grain of sand with this new awareness of its essence. Each day I walked in this way and each day I came close to a fuller understanding of the message. I had asked for a gift and it was given.

Mexico, Serenity

Clarity is easy here in this little fishing village by the sea where life is lived simply and quietly, where the seconds, minutes, hours of the day are open wide to emptiness of purpose so new thoughts can filter in. No distractions whatsoever! So I write and swim and sunbathe, walk the beach and meet friends there for dinner, watching the brilliant sunsets and the red orange sun plopping into the ocean each night. Yes, it does plop and very quickly, right off the edge of the earth.

Nourish Your Soul

Good Morning dear Frieda and Valto, would you please share your thoughts as I begin my writing today?

"Good morning, we are here with you now as you love your peaceful day. You forgot to say you are at your sacred writing table; your glass of clear water at hand and the whole day stretching freshly out before you waiting

to be filled with whatever you desire. This is the joy of what you have created during your life—to be able to sit back and relax without all the pressing details of a life built on endless activity. This is a blessing that life does not mean ceaselessly, endlessly creating for the sake of some meaningless title or reward. We understand this is important for self-esteem and future entitlement but it is the inner-self, the life of the eternal soul that requires the nourishment. Hold fast to what you are doing and growing. Your light, a part of loves light, will be caught and held and made true for all who understand and create with this same light that you offer. Love is indeed the heart of the Universe. We will always help you bring it into fruition for others."

This Book

Now that our book is almost completed will it be successful in giving connection to people?

> *"Yes, it is easily transferred at different levels. Stay true to what you have received and know. This is your experience. Tell your readers from your heart what is your truth. Stand back of these writings and your belief in yourself as the receiver. These messages were not given without knowing that you are the right person."*

Meditation Happiness and Contentment

I sat on the couch, closed my eyes breathing deeply, experiencing that drawing inward feeling that has become so familiar. Breathed again in and out, going deeper, letting the cleansing bubbling brook rush through my body over little tinkling stones. Such a releasing contented feeling with the little wavelets sweeping and swirling over mossy rocks. Inwardly listening to the watery, rushing music while purple white light played softly behind my eyes. Happiness began to shimmer through me, my lips curved up into the little happy smile I love to know is there, a sure sign love is present. Happiness was obviously the theme because I felt happy from head to toe. I just felt delightfully happy. Nothing else, just happy, happy, happy. I sat for a while breathing it in and breathing it out, breathing in and breathing out. It felt soooo good, so restful, why ever leave this perfect bliss? No needs, no wants, just happy. Sitting, absorbing, being joyfully happy.

Spiritual Connection

Would you talk about spiritual connection again please?

> *"It is a link, a thread of knowledge to your invisible Source. It cannot be broken once created. It is forever available. The link connects you to knowledge not available on planet earth and is totally loving and enriching for both mind and body. Link yourself more completely to our love to carry you forward to the path that you have opened as an author and an artist and a healer of people with the writings."*

Spiritual Guides

This morning I asked for more information about spiritual guides.

> *"We walk with you and talk with you and guide you internally but we are outside also, coming from other realms far away from yours. Ours is a world of great beauty, the beauty you feel in your heart during meditations. You feel our breath of love as it vibrates through your body, never ceasing. Keep expressing it in, expressing it out, glowing it outward. Creating for everyone on planet earth a way to be in the vibrating center of love. Breathe it in, breathe it out. Create your new lives on earth from within its brilliant flame."*

GLOSSARY

Altar of Attunement: Attune physically to the magic of the altar we have been given as a symbol for growth.

Balance: Balance our divine and human natures to release earth's bounty to provide for all.

Birth: We were each given human consciousness, God's living Presence in the soul, and our own free will.

Creation: Begins with a thought that expands outwards through vibrations of electrical energy from All That Is. All thought is a form of creation.

Death: After death the promise is for the expansion of our earth life at another higher level within the infinite Universe. After death we go on living.

Destiny of Perfection: Create with inner spiritual guidance, love for ourselves, and our planet to continually raise earth's ability to absorb what it needs.

Divine Connection: Each person is born with a permanent connection to the vast knowledge and guidance of the divine Universe.

Ego/Personality: Our outer presentation to the world that holds and directs all our beliefs about ourselves.

Free Will: Given at birth. We each have the freedom to express ourselves without reservation.

Golden Principles: A set of eight standards for peaceful coexistence.

Higher Self: Our divine inner link.

Ions: A group of atoms that carry a positive or negative electric charge.

Inner Peace: Believing and knowing that we are connected to the loving Source of all creation, and that we are guided throughout life.

Intuition: Inner master teachers who travel with each person through life.

God: The Source of all life that is within everything, knowable in mind and heart, both formless and visible in everything we see, All that Is.

Guides: We are guided even when we do not ask. We may have one or many guarding and protecting us.

Health: Be mindful of our relationships, the food and drink we place in our bodies and our thoughts. When the body is weak the entire bodily system is disrupted.

Heaven and Hell: We create our own heaven and personal hell.

Judgment: There are no limits, no judgments except our own for right or wrong action.

Law of Individual Creation: Give into the dynamic pulsing force of creative energy for the good of all and good shall be returned in full measure.

Law of Money: Money flows to all who ask strongly, repetitively and directly.

Master Plan of Perfection: Our inner knowledge of right conduct that is within the core-self, the conscience, and the intuition.

Mother Ship of All Knowledge: A colossal divine complex of perfect beauty and light that was our original home.

Pain and Suffering: It is intended to identify and examine imbalances within the body.

Planet Earth: A school of knowledge where we can utilize all available physical, mental and spiritual resources.

Prayer: All supplication is the request for release from a measure of darkness into the goodness and sweetness of light. Consistent prayer can lead to an awakening of our connection with God.

Righteous Choices: Peace, harmony, love, equality, the giving of ourselves to raise the consciousness of neighboring territories and our nation into brotherhood with all others.

Soul: Inner core of the self, the seed center of all knowledge, the mastermind, the control center. Often called the seed-heart-center or crystal-seed-center.

Soul Consciousness: The raising of strong wavelengths of positive magnetic energy throughout the world with loving inner work. In this lifetime there is advancement in soul consciousness throughout the planet.

Stream of Consciousness Writing: Contact with higher vibrations to receive messages.

Subconscious: The inner-self that is hidden inner knowledge from our crystal-seed-center, the soul.

Universal Intelligence: The vast intelligence that is available to all and only limited by our lack of belief and application to learn.

BIBLIOGRAPHY

Arrien, Angeles. Signs of Life: The Five Universal Shapes and How to Use Them. Arcus Publishing Company, 1992.

Armstrong, Jack. Lessons from the Source: A Spiritual Guidebook for Navigating Life's Journey. iUniverse, 2008.

Bach. Richard. Illusions: The Adventures of a Reluctant Messiah. Delacourte Press, 1977.

Bolen, Jean Shinoda. The Tao of Psychology: Synchronicity And The Self. Harper & Row 1979.

Cameron, Julia. The Artist's Way: A Spiritual Path to Higher Creativity. Tarcher/Perigee Books, 1992.

Canan, Janine. Message from Amma: In the Language of The Heart. Celestial Arts, 2004.

Castillejo, Irene Claremont de. Knowing Woman: A Feminine Psychology. Harper Colophon, 1974.

Chopra, Deepak. How to Know God: The Soul's Journey into the Mystery of Mysteries. Three Rivers Press, 2000.

Chopra, Deepak. Creating Health: How to Wake up the Body's Intelligence. Houghton Mifflin Company, 1991.

Clark, Glenn. The Man Who Tapped The Secrets Of The Universe. The University of Science and Philosophy, 2006.

Dalai Lama. Live in a Better Way. My Brothers Publishing Company, 1999.

Eadie, Betty, Embraced by the Light. Gold leaf Press, 1992.

Edwards, Gill. Stepping Into The Magic: A New Approach to Everyday Life. Judy Piatkus ltd of London, 1993.

Emery, Marcia. The Intuitive Healer: Accessing Your Inner Physician. St. Martin's Griffin, 2000.

Fersen, Eugene. Science of Being. J. F. Tapley Company, 1923.

Fersen, Eugene. Science of Being: Twenty seven lessons, Eugene Fersen, 1927.

Frawley, David. Ayurveda and the Mind: The Healing of Consciousness. Lotus Press, 1992.

Gangaji with Moore, Roslyn. Just Like You: An autobiography. DO Publishing, 2003.

Gawain, Shakti. Developing Intuition: Practical Guidance for Daily Life. New World Library, 2000.

Holmes, Ernest. Science of Mind. Dodd Mead & Company, 1938.

Holmes, Ernest. Living the Science of Mind. DeVorss & Company, 1991.

Jung, C. G. Memories, Dreams, Reflections. Vintage books, 1965.

Jung, Carl G. Man and his Symbols. Aldus Books Limited, 1979.

Kelder, Peter. Ancient Secret of the Fountain of Youth, Book 2. Doubleday, 1999.

Kolbenschlag, Madonna. Kiss Sleeping Beauty Good-Bye. Bantam Books, 1981.

Meadows, Kenneth. Shamanic Spirit: A Practical Guide to Personal Fulfillment. Bear & Company, 2004.

Metzner, Ralph. The Unfolding Self: Varieties of Transformative Experience. Origin Press, 1998.

Myss, Caroline. Anatomy of The Spirit: The Seven Stages of Power and Healing. Three rivers Press, 1996.

Muktananda, Swami. Meditate. State University of New York Press, 1991.

Orloff, Judith, M.D. Second Sight: An Intuitive Psychiatrist tells her Extraordinary Story and Show's you how to Tap your own Inner Wisdom. Three Rivers Press, 2010.

Reed, Henry. Edgar Cayce: On Channeling your Higher Self. Warners Books Inc, 1989.

Roman, Sanaya and Packer, Duane. Opening To Channel: How to Connect With Your Guide. H J Kramer Inc, 1987.

Russell, Walter. The Message of The Divine Illiad. W.R. Foundation, 1949.

Sanford, Agnes. The Healing Light. Macalester Park, 1947.

Stein, Diane. All Women Are Healers: A Comprehensive Guide To Natural Healing. The Crossing Press, 1990.

Tolle, Eckhart. The Power of Now: A Guide to Spiritual Enlightenment. Namaste Publishing and New World Library, 2004.

Walsch, Neale Donald. Conversations with God: an uncommon dialogue, Book 1. G. P. Putnam's Sons, 1996.

Wolf, Kristine. The Way: a Novel. Crown Publishers, 2011.

ABOUT THE AUTHOR

Lin Lipetz received her Master of Fine Arts degree in Painting and Ceramics from the University of Washington and a Bachelor of Science degree from San Jose State University in Interior Architecture. She has been an established visual artist and art educator for many years.

Twenty-five years ago a profound spiritual awakening gradually transformed her life and her worldview. Through Dialogues with the Universe she received many powerful messages that she recorded knowing they should be shared with the world. She has written this book to present many of these Dialogues and the poems written by her invisible spiritual guides, plus the illuminating way of transformation that she has been given. She says, "The Secret of Inner Presence is a book of love, written in collaboration with the Universe, for all those who seek higher wisdom to transcend and transform their lives and possibly the global community. When the gift of Inner Presence was given to me, without a strong religious or spiritual background, it proved that everyone has this power within, just waiting to be awakened through the gentle power of peaceful love."

She teaches this Awakening process through Meditation, Stream of Consciousness Writing, and Dialogues with the Universe during scheduled workshops and lectures. If you would like to be on her mailing list to receive more information please go to her author website, www.secretofinnerpresence.com. To view many of her Intuitive Paintings please go to her artist website, www.linlipetz.com.

She lives in the heart of the wine country, Sonoma, California, where she paints, writes, teaches visual art, and leads The Secret of Inner Presence workshops.